"Donald White has put this outstanding thousands of business owners he knows moving through the transition process of selling or stepping back from their businesses. Don is a man of the highest integrity, and his clients and colleagues listen when he speaks. He has spoken all over the world about real topics that make you think, reflect, and get on with the job!"

—Angus McQueen
CEO, McQueen Group

"For any seasoned financial services practitioner who has yet to both declare and have a written business transition strategy for their business, this book is a must. Don provides a personal and very applicable business view to the most important things which need to be considered when thinking about your own exit strategy—long before you intend on such a transition."

—Jim Brownlee, CFP, CLU, ChFC
Vice President Independent Distribution
Canada Life Assurance Company

"I found this book to be both honest and thought-provoking. Thank you for your insight and the wisdom of your experience. I am now motivated to plan for succession for myself and my clients."

—Randy Reed, CPA
Managing Partner, Reed & Company CPA Firm

"Any business owner (or someone who is inspired to become one) should read this book. From start to finish, I was captivated by the stories and didn't want to put the book down. I only wish this book was written three years earlier before we sold our business (to my kids). Informative, educational, inspiring, a great benefit to all who read. It really had me thinking about how I ran my business. Don's success came because he always put the customer first."

—Nick Fiorella
Founder, Fiorella Insurance

"This book is a must-read for any entrepreneur building a business and creating a legacy. Don has done a masterful job in sharing the many lessons he learned while exiting his business, and he is giving back through the gift of sharing. This book is a no-nonsense guide to help other business owners avoid the many pitfalls of succession and legacy transfers. I wish I had this book to hand out to the hundreds of business owners I have had the pleasure of working with over my 30-year career in the financial services industry."

—Jeffery A. Ferguson
Senior Executive Leader, Financial Services Industry

"The 'D-Man' is one of the finest and most intellectually honest men I have had the honor to professionally support over the past two decades. In his book, Don shares his 25-year personal mission of executing a win/win succession plan for all stakeholders in his business. He clearly outlines simple steps to build and launch a successful succession plan. His masterful grip and practical understanding of this topic lends itself to any industry or professional organization—not just within the world of finance and advisory firms. I have been a witness to Don living a purposeful life and building his legacy as a trusted leader. My life has been blessed to know him professionally and personally. Now, the world gets to know him, too!"

—Patty Azar
Founder & Former CEO, Vision Alignment, Inc.

"Building a business is like building a home—all the steps should be done in order. Don White convincingly lays out all the critical elements to building a business upon these critical building blocks that will allow a business to last for generations and succeed when others cease."

—Jim Rogers, MBA, CFP
Retired Financial Services Executive; Past President
Million Dollar Round Table (2008)

"Don's personal life journey is thoughtfully shared to highlight how every ending brings a new beginning. With the goal of successfully transitioning his business, he leaves the reader with his life's legacy: Move your business forward with confidence and purpose with the ultimate goal of putting others first: your clients, your staff, your family, and finally, you. With over 40 years in the Financial Services business, Don has vast knowledge and experience in what matters most: purpose, gratitude, time, health, and surrounding yourself with the people you cherish the most."

—Jennifer A. Borislow
President, Borislow Insurance; Past President
Million Dollar Round Table (2012)

"This is a book every entrepreneur needs to read. Business schools do a wonderful job teaching students how to start, build, and grow an enterprise, but virtually nothing on the topic of business continuity and succession that Don White tackles masterfully in his new book. I highly recommend it!"

—Bud Jordan
Retired Financial Services Industry Executive

"Don has shared his wisdom and knowledge for anyone wanting to position their business for sale. The difference between knowledge and wisdom is experience, and Don has years of experience. Whether you intend to sell in the next year or have just started, his advice is to build a practice you would be proud to sell. Our profession is filled with those who are very successful solo practitioners and then wake up tired and losing clients in their late 60's. Heed the awesome advice, read the entire book as if it was written just for you, and succeed in the goal of beginning with the end in mind!"

—Brian D. Heckert
Founder and CEO, FSM Wealth, Inc.; MDRT Past President 2016

"Don has accumulated a wealth of wisdom and expertise, having spent more than 40 years as a financial advisor helping clients achieve their life goals. He's also a highly successful business owner who took the time to plan his succession, and now he's sharing how he did it and what he learned in a great first book. I highly recommend it for any entrepreneur who has not yet planned for the end of their business journey."

—Dan Arnold
CEO, LPL Financial

"Donald White has written a must-read for newbies and veterans alike. If you're looking forward or looking back, this book has something to say to you about making your life and your life's work count."

—Solomon Hicks, Author & Speaker
Founder/CEO of Hicks Global Enterprises

"Small business is the single most important generator of wealth in America, but without a succession plan, it is fool's gold. Donald White has beautifully laid out the steps you need to take to turn your small business into a positive legacy. It is a must-read for all small business entrepreneurs!"

—Patricia J. Abram
Former Chief Marketing Officer
American Skandia Life & Mutual Service Corporation

"Our vision of helping others as financial advisors is dwarfed by the realities of getting by until the unexpected bittersweet end slams into our unprepared world long after our proper time to pass our torch does. Donald's masterfully delivered storytelling and smooth weave of quotes, scripture, and experience in this must-read for all successful financial advisors remind us of the importance captured in his chosen title. May your choices in life and business always lead to the blessings of new beginnings."

—Stephen Kagawa
CEO, The Pacific Bridge Companies

"In his book, *Always End with the Beginning in Mind*, Don explains in great detail using many examples on how to leverage everything you've built and how to transition its continuation to guide the successor's purchase into a sustainable healthy business. I've had the privilege of knowing Don for many years, and this book brings to the reader all he has seen, experienced, and heard from those business owners to give all who read this book hope and a vision for the future."

—Tony Barletta
Former Professional Baseball Player; Founder, Brightway Insurance

"This is an excellent read, informative and original, thoughtful. A must-read for owners/principals of a financial planning practice. When it comes to business succession in advisory, many planners work like cobblers—they repair everyone else's shoes but their own! I can validate these events as a wholesaler for 30 years; Don delivers critical advice in a practical manner."

—Jackson Langford
Director, Financial Wholesaler/Trustee

"Before I even finished the book, I [knew] anyone starting a business should read it. The author presents his business life experience and then lists positive and negative actions one can take to build a thriving business. Finding the right people is key in any business, and the insight presented into human behavior gives the reader a great tool for hiring. In short, if you are starting a business, this book should be the first step."

—Joe Wertheim
Entrepreneur

"*Always End with the Beginning in Mind* relates Don White's journey of successfully transitioning his business to the next generation. Through his wonderful business career, Don walks us through how difficult it is to make a succession plan work for all the parties involved. Any business owner(s) can create a succession plan, but it takes a lot of thought, a lot of time, a lot of trial and error, a lot of persistence, and most importantly, getting the right successor team in place."

—Julian H. Good Jr., CLU, ChFC, AEP
Past President, Million Dollar Round Table (2011)
CEO, Good Financial Group

"I don't know about you, but I've read far too many books written by people who have clearly never lived the life—or had the success—they advocate. By contrast, *Always End with the Beginning in Mind* is real and relevant, authored by one of the most authentic people I have ever had the honor of knowing. In this fabulous book, Don provides us with a 'toolkit' of fascinating insights and practical tips on succession planning, with ideas taken from over 40 years of experience in a wonderful profession. An absolute must-read!"

—Sandro Forte, FCII, CSP, FPSA, FPFS
CEO, Forte Financial Group; Professional Speaker & Author

"Don White is an amazing communicator and strategist who will lead you to new beginnings. Read this book and discover the tools necessary to end well in business and in your life."

—Dr. Raymond Underwood
Chief Encouragement Officer, Family Church Network

"Donald White has written a primer that cleverly navigates the perilous journey of a seamless transition of leadership for the small business you built from scratch. Specific, well-organized gems of wisdom gleaned over the years, backed by numerous and often funny or profound illustrations, make this book educational, entertaining, and a no-brainer for those early in their career. Practical but fun. Don't miss it!"

—Mark Hughes, MD, FAAEM, FACEP

"Don's willingness to show me the ropes and invite me into client relationships catapulted me into a career that I have now loved for over 20 years. His book demonstrates that the best way for a young advisor to succeed is to have a generous mentor. Don was that person for me. I saw his generosity towards me and others up close, and it still stands as one of my favorite qualities about him. As you'll see in the book, even though our time together ended in a way no one could have expected, his humility and self-awareness went a long way to helping us reconcile. Of all the mentors I've had, Don was by far the most generous to me with his time and money. I'm eternally grateful to him."

—Steve Scalici
Financial Advisor & Don White's Former Business Partner

"If you care about your clients, staff, reputation, then succession planning matters a lot. *In Always End with the Beginning in Mind*, Don White shows how to use accumulated years of relational capital, make our own good luck, and how to find a successor that will continue the values and vision we spent so many years developing in our firms. I especially like the last chapter on leadership. Here, Don instills the confidence that just as I am the one who was needed to build my business, I am the right person to lead, passing it on to my successor. As a bonus, Don is a great storyteller, and he writes with authenticity from his years of experience and a life given to encouraging others in reaching their goals."

—**Jude McDaniel, CLU, ChFC, AIF**
Managing Partner, McDaniel Knutson Financial Partners

"I was honored to have the opportunity to read an advance copy of Don's book. During my career, I have purchased several businesses from founders and have transitioned many management teams. In this book, Don makes many points that I learned the hard way, and he does so in a flowing style full of insight and stories. If you are a founder and thinking of one day transferring your business to a successor, this book is a great read and will set you on the path for a successful transition. If you have not thought about succession planning or do not see its value, this book is an absolute must-read."

—**Alan Dahl**
Director, Advisor, and Retired HealthCare Executive

"A great read packed heavily with must-know information and insights any and every entrepreneur can glean from. Although I don't doubt that many business owners have begun their careers without the end in mind, White makes an irrefutable case for all successful owners, having recognized that their success came from God, and as good stewards, their responsibility is to allow him to find their 'Joshua' and end with the beginning in mind."

—**David Engesath**
Founder of Rare Earth Pottery

"Don has put his years of experience and knowledge into the guidelines and recommendations he makes in his new book, *Always End with the Beginning in Mind*. As I read his comments and thoughts on succession planning, it made me think of the many issues I had to deal with in my career as a producer, leader, and CEO. He is on target with his guidance and suggestions for how to plan for the sale of your organization while transferring the company to new owners and bowing out gracefully from the daily routines of running the company and taking care of the needs of the clients. This is an entertaining and easy to read book filled with excellent suggestions we should all be using in planning for the sale of our practices."

—**Marvin H. Feldman, CLU, ChFC**
CEO, Feldman Financial Group and the LIFE Foundation (retired)
Past MDRT President (2003)

Always end with the Beginning in Mind

How a Firm Remains Great After the Founder Exits

Donald F. White

Made for Success
PUBLISHING

Made for Success Publishing
P.O. Box 1775 Issaquah, WA 98027
www.MadeForSuccessPublishing.com

Distributed by Made for Success Publishing

First Printing

Library of Congress Cataloging-in-Publication data
White, Donald F.
      ALWAYS END WITH THE BEGINNING IN MIND: How a Firm
      Remains Great After the Founder Exits:
          p. cm.

      LCCN: 2019939284
      ISBN: 978-1-64146-381-2 (*Paperback*)
      ISBN: 978-1-64146-610-3 (*Hardback*)
      ISBN: 978-1-64146-520-5 (*Audiobook*)
      ISBN: 978-1-64146-543-4 (*eBook*)

Printed in the United States of America

For further information contact Made for Success Publishing
+14255266480 or email service@madeforsuccess.net

To the three most important people in my life
—Grace, Sydney and Reagan

CONTENTS

"WHAT DO I DO NOW?"

This is a question asked sooner or later by all who have built private businesses, particularly those in the financial services arena.

They've put in years of effort, care, concern, wins and losses, and personnel, client, and financial challenges. Their business practice has survived, grown, and finally thrived … but as father time winds down, a clock that no one outruns, the question hangs overhead.

The very fact that the vast majority of practitioners who have built successful businesses have not addressed the matter of transition, but rather have simply defaulted to a future position of cessation instead of thinking about and planning for their succession is alarming.

This appears reason enough for my good friend, Don White, to have written this perspective on not only what lies ahead, but also to share a myriad of factors that come into play with regard to making a decision to address the subject, and take action.

If you are thinking about what to do about an associate, a successor for your business, or a transition plan that may take effect this year or years hence, this is the book for you to read, absorb, digest, and *act upon*.

To his credit, Don has "been there and done that." He has played many different roles during his outstanding career in the world of finance as a salesman, manager, business owner, and financial advisor.

In this, his first book, he does not disappoint. It is packed with analogies, examples, stories, real-life experiences, and philosophical gems that invite the reader to reflect upon what they have done, are doing, and may end up with at the conclusion of their business journey.

Don does not sugarcoat what is required to accurately assess what needs to be done. He leads the reader step-by-step as to what is necessary to end *well*. The process he describes over the various chapters is easy to absorb yet packs a punch with truth everyone needs to hear, regardless of where they are in their journey.

If you are a business owner, particularly in the world of financial services, or are planning on buying a business book in the coming year, I encourage you to take the time to heed these principles, as someday you will end your journey—hopefully, with the beginning in mind.

Bruce Etherington, BA, CLU ChFC, CFP
Author, Speaker, and Chairman of Etherington & Associates
Mississauga, Ontario, Canada

"Great is the art of beginning, but greater the art is of ending."
—Henry Wadsworth Longfellow

I WILL NOT BE THAT GUY

After over 40 years in the financial services business, it is my conservative estimate that I have attended upward of 300 various and sundry conferences of one form or another, either as a delegate and/or a speaker. While some of these events are intraday, most conferences last three to five days. To hear or be present at five to eight speeches from multiple speakers per day would be expected. If you are doing the math, that means, conservatively, I have participated in over 5,000 presentations in my career. Most of the speeches are long forgotten, but there is one that is forever burned into my memory.

When you arrive at most conventions, you receive an agenda. The agenda gives you a synopsis of each talk and the speaker's credentials, along with when and where the speech will take place. The "main platform" speeches, which everyone can attend, are placed in order on the day they will be given. The "breakouts," which are typically longer and take a deeper dive on a specific topic, are bunched together by date and time, and each attendee has the option of choosing one.

Several years ago, my wife and I were attending an MDRT Top of the Table (TOT) meeting. TOT is a great conference. The speakers are incredible, and the attendees are limited to a few hundred of the highest-producing financial advisors from around the world. Most of the main platform speakers are paid professionals, but virtually all the breakouts feature talks from some of the best and brightest advisors in the world. This meeting was no exception.

Scanning the agenda, one breakout session caught my eye. Entitled, *Generations of Success*, the description read, "A solid succession plan could be the key to your business longevity. Hear from multi-generational practices, including familial legacies, to help develop successful strategies to bridge both age and cultural gaps. Learn the keys to smoothing over differences, developing a comprehensive and agreed-upon plan and, most importantly, how to let go of a cherished business."

I saw the session would be moderated by a well-known advisor who had purchased a large advisory firm from its founder several years prior. He would be leading an international panel discussion with a long-time TOT member and his son, as well as another member and his daughter from overseas. This had all the makings of an unforgettable presentation—one you did not want to miss.

Business continuity and succession planning have become hot subjects over the past several years as the Baby Boomers continue to age. In 2020, the average age of a financial advisor in the United States was over 50 (and continues to go up). Less than 12% of advisors were under the age of 35[1]. In my observation, among the most successful advisors, the average age—and certainly the median age—is even higher. This subject of an aging advisor population is on everyone's radar. The number of financial advisors who die or are limited by medical issues while still practicing is reaching an epidemic. According to a report done annually by Cerulli and Associates, over a third of practices will change hands in the 2020s, whether the advisor likes it or not. As such, this subject has piqued the industry's interest for many years.

Shoemakers Fix Your Own Shoes!

My career path began as a life insurance agent, and even after our firm expanded to include investment management and advisory in the 1990s, life insurance has always been a major emphasis of the firm. Consequently, it is routine to discuss succession planning with our clients.

- *How long do you want to continue working?*
- *What are your thoughts about retirement?*
- *Do you have someone in place who could lead the firm if you either live too long, die too soon, or become disabled?*

For most businesspeople, their single largest asset is their business, and what becomes of their largest asset is a huge deal. They are asking themselves:

- *Do I want to sell the business?*
- *Do I want to turn the business over to one or more of my children? If so, who leads the operation?*
- *Do I have an in-house successor, or do I have an agreement to merge with a competitor I trust?*
- *If not, am I simply going to let the company wither away until it falls by the wayside?*

Everyone knows that there is only one thing certain in life—everybody dies—and making provision for death, disability, and retirement is simply not optional. Unless, I guess, you are a financial advisor!

Financial advisors love to discuss business continuity with their customers, but advisors do a horrible job of advising themselves. It is a classic case of *"shoemaker fix your own shoes."* For many advisors, a succession plan for themselves is apparently of little importance.

In any case, the *Generations of Success* session appeared intriguing. It looked like the people scheduled to speak had actually completed and implemented a plan for their succession. Based on the standing-room-only attendance, the subject had created significant interest among the attendees.

From the earliest days, our firm intentionally recruited with an eye toward succession. However, a lack of understanding of the process, coupled with bad decision making, led to a string of recruits leaving for other opportunities. Frankly, the whole process had made me a bit gun-shy, but the line in the description for the meeting, "… learn the keys to smoothing over differences and developing an agreed-upon plan" caught my attention fully. As Renee Zellweger's character in *Jerry Maguire* famously said, "[They] had me at hello."

No Succession Here!

The moderator did a good job of steering the conversation. However, as I listened, one thing became painfully obvious—the only one on the stage who was part of an executed succession plan was the moderator! Unlike his panelists, he had succeeded his senior partner in their company and was now leading his firm. The advertising of the session had led me to believe the panelists were there to discuss how they implemented a successful transfer of their respective businesses to a new generation. As it turns out, nothing could be farther from the truth.

Both fathers, well into their 70s, had neither relinquished control nor were they letting go of the reins… at least not any time soon[2]. Then, something profound hit me. These firms were prospering *despite* the involvement of the fathers, not *because of* it. Indeed, their appointed successors, their adult children, *were* the reason for the continued growth in the firm. The current success of the business was no longer being influenced by their fathers, regardless of their continued involvement within the company.

I started squirming in my chair, hoping I was simply misreading the fathers. The more they spoke, the more obvious it became neither of the fathers, at least in their own minds, had transferred their firms to the people sitting next to them on stage. When the moderator asked them if they intended to retire, they both just smiled. One went on to say, "Retire? I am having too much fun!"

Internally, I was screaming, "Yeah, but is it fun for everyone else? Is it *fun* for your clients and customers? Is this *fun* for your staff? Above all, is it *fun* for your adult children?"

It did not appear either child looked like they were having *fun* listening to their fathers hold court! In fact, one of the children (who were hardly children any longer) could not contain an audible gasp as the father pontificated about the fun he was having. It seemed like a massive misrepresentation. These adult children had not succeeded anyone. Instead, the fathers had merely employed their respective son and daughter to manage the existing clientele and build their own book of business. Unconsciously, I turned to the person sitting next to me, who I did not know from Adam nor could I pick out of a lineup, and said, "I will *not* be that guy!"

It was obvious that both the daughter and the son were completely capable of running these respective firms. However, there was one clear difference between them and the moderator. The moderator was not related to the founder he succeeded. He had executed an arms-length, straightforward transaction with his business partner. Money had changed hands, and, at a point in time, the founder was out, and the successor was in.

For the first time, I really understood why passing a business down to the next generation is so difficult and frequently unsuccessful—the second generation rarely has *skin in the game*. David Kauppi wrote an article in 2014 for Business Know-How entitled *Passing Your Business to the Next*

Generation, where he said, "Although it is a noble gesture, passing a business down to the next generation is more often than not, unsuccessful. In fact, statistics show that only one-third of all family businesses are successfully transferred to the next generation and only 13% are transferred onto the third generation."

He went on to say, "Many family business consultants say the primary reason for this low survival rate is the failure to develop and effectively plan for the transfer of ownership and management of the closely held family business… [While] I agree [that] the low survival rate is [often] the failure to develop and effectively plan for the transfer of ownership and management of the closely held family business, in my dealing with family businesses, I find that there are some more fundamental reasons. The first is that the next generation has a lot different lifestyle than the business founder and entrepreneur. They do not share the same drive and commitment that dad needed to build the business from scratch. They go to the good schools, get a taste of the good life and generally do not share the passion of the business founder."[3]

Because neither of these fathers had executed an arms-length agreement with their children and money had not changed hands, the dads felt entitled, if not obligated, to continue running their company—even though it may or may not be in the best interest of their clients, employees, children, or themselves. One of my early mentors in the business once told me, "Always do what is in the best interest of the person sitting in front of you, and your interest will always take care of itself." While I find most great businesspeople believe in this adage as it applies to the way they treat their customers, it does not necessarily carry over to the way they treat their own businesses.

I left the session more determined than ever to create a succession plan for our firm that would work. At the time, I had no idea how providence would play a role in making it come to pass, but I knew, without a shadow of a doubt, that building a business with the intent of selling that business is best for the clients, first and foremost. It is also best for the employees, successor, and founder, in that order.

CHAPTER 1

PROVIDENCE

I n 2005, Steve Magallanes—who I like to call Mags—applied to be an intern for us. He was an undergraduate at Palm Beach Atlantic University in West Palm Beach, Florida. My partner, and presumed successor, was a PBAU alum and was instrumental in steering business students to work as interns for us. Most of these students worked for three to six months and left. Mags was different. He interned for us for over a year, and when he graduated, he joined the firm full-time. Although he left for about a year to work in his family's business, he returned and became one of our key employees. After my partner and I parted ways, I approached Mags about being my successor. His response was priceless.

"I've seen the boss's job ... and I don't want it."

While Mags is a phenomenal advisor, he does not enjoy what my business coach, Patty Azar, likes to call *the business of the business*. He enjoys advising clients but has no interest in the mundane workings of running a business. He wants to do his job of giving quality advice to his clients and go home at night to be with his wife and four little ones. Nevertheless, he did encourage me in my search by saying, "If you find someone who loves the business side and will leave me alone on the advisory side, I am all in."

Providence At Work

I am a big believer in providence. I am convinced everything in life is interconnected, and things happen for a reason, whether good or bad. To say I was devastated when my business partner and I split up would be an understatement. The irony is, I love Steve Scalici. He is unquestionably one of the finest people I have ever met. Unfortunately, as much as I hate to admit it, I was the reason he left. I took advantage of him and our relationship. My insolence led him to leave and associate elsewhere. Knowing I was the one responsible for Steve moving on haunted me for years.

While the relationship between spouses is revered, the relationship between friends can be more sacrosanct. Steve Scalici became my associate at the tender age of 25. He was the protégé every businessperson would want. He is incredibly smart. His work ethic is exceptional. He is always looking out for the best interests of others. He has what the Scriptures call the *mind of Christ*.[1] He chooses not to operate out of selfishness or vain conceit. His humility is what attracts people. Being a master of successfully juxtaposing your own interests with the interests of others is the epitome of a servant-leader.

It seems nearly incongruous, therefore, that I could mess up a relationship like that … but I am capable of almost anything. When it comes to screwing up a relationship, it seems I have mastered the art; and with Steve, I screwed up royally. Steve not only had the right to leave, but he left because he loved *me* too much to stay. Steve was the exact person I wanted to succeed me in the business. Unfortunately, he was not the *right* person to succeed me.

Now, I am not suggesting you make the mistakes I made and run amazing people off. What I am suggesting is that you need to be aware the person you think is the *best* person to succeed you may in fact not be the *right* person at all. The founder brings in this amazing, albeit wrong person to succeed them (or elevates said amazing wrong person to their level of incompetence), and the entire business ends up going down in flames shortly after the founder steps aside. Thankfully for Steve and me, my initial succession plan failed.

Back in the 1960s, Laurence Peter, a Canadian sociologist, wrote *The Peter Principle*. What Dr. Peter's research found was just because an employee stands out in one position does not mean they will excel at another. In fact, employers frequently elevate people with what Peter famously called a promotion to their "level of incompetence" and suffer the inevitable consequences associated with the decision. Dr. Peter concluded an employee's inability to perform at a high level in one position after excelling in another might result less from general incompetence on the part of the employee, but more likely, they simply do not possess the skills needed to succeed in their new position. It is not so much a case of the person being incompetent, but rather they are merely not suited for the role.

One of Peter's famous statements was rather than cream rising to the top, "cream rises until it sours."[2] Almost inevitably, this leads to organizations made up almost entirely of people inadequate for the tasks they are assigned to fulfill. George Barna, in his book, *If Things are So Good, Why Do They Feel So Bad,* penned, "Peter wrote, 'The cream rises until it sours,' in 1969. A quarter-century later, America is drowning in a sea of soured cream."[3] And I would suggest, now a half-century later, the drowning continues.

After Steve left, he joined a team at a major wirehouse. This move allowed him to become the founder of a church in Jupiter, Florida. He is an unpaid pastor of a congregation, impacting lives in countless ways while at the same time earning his living advising clients at the brokerage house. Steve was not supposed to be the owner/operator of an independent financial services operation. This would not have allowed him the time to be a pastor who is changing hundreds, if not thousands, of lives.

Steve has a calling, and it is only partially as a financial advisor. Frankly, I was too insolent at the time to see he was better served *not* being with the firm than being with us. That is a hard statement to say out loud, but it is nonetheless true. The foundational tenet of our firm is to always do what is in the best interest of the person in front of us. When I was a recruit with the old E.F. Hutton & Company, my manager, who was the chief advocate of this principle, instilled two ideas that became guiding principles in my career for the many decades thereafter.

The first was, "Nothing happens until someone sells somebody something!" We will discuss more about this in another part of the book. The second is this founding tenet: "Always do what is in the best interest of the person sitting in front of you, and your interest will always take care of itself."

> *"Always do what is in the best interest of the person sitting in front of you, and your interest will always take care of itself."*

These two principles became the foundation of our business. However, the latter principle applies just as surely to staff, associates, and especially to a successor, as it does to clientele. It may or may not be in a person's best interest to be a successor. Some founders may need several people to succeed them.

Just because someone is a great founder does not mean they can take an organization to the next level. I saw this in our church. My wife, Grace, and I have been associated with Treasure Coast Community

Church (TC3) since its inception. TC3 started with eight families meeting in a house a couple of times a week in the early 1990s. It has grown organically to become the second-largest congregation in our community, with its own campus and thousands of congregants. The founding pastor was outstanding. However, once the church had grown to about 200, he (not the church) hit *his* ceiling of complexity, and the church started to dismantle. To his credit, he recognized what was happening and stepped down.

I remember thinking at the time, *how does someone stop being a pastor?* Are you not supposed to just keep gutting it out no matter what? The short answer is no. He stepped down to pursue his dream of being a counselor, but also because his work at TC3 was done. He opened the door for the next generation of leadership to grow what he had sown. What seemed rocky ground to the founder was fertile soil for his successor. As a result, the church has prospered and is far more effective since the founder left.

No one can say what the best solution is for any organization, no less the one you may run. However, if you are open to the myriad of possibilities, you may find the direction you initially thought was best was not right because what is *right* is far too easy to confuse with what you think is *best*.

What Not to Do

TCFin is the short version of Treasure Coast Financial Services, Inc., the original name of our company. TCFin was originally to be the conduit for an enterprise my original business partner, Bud Jordan, and I started to facilitate a life insurance distribution system for Prudential-Bache Securities in the state of Florida. Started in 1988, within six years, the venture had run its course. Bud and I made the fateful decision to allow me to buy him out. My dream was to convert the enterprise into an independent financial services business where if a client had a question involving money, they would start by calling us. The objective was to be our client's point of contact when it came to financial matters. Some matters, like life insurance and investments, we would handle. For others, we would help them find the right person or firm to resolve their other needs.

Before operating TCFin as a full-service planning and investment management firm, I logged 18 years of prior experience that included time as a life insurance agent and manager, failed business owner (not once, but twice), and stints working with two different investment houses helping to expand their life insurance capacity. Suffice it to say, by the time TCFin became an independent financial services company, I had quite an extensive background that served me well as an entrepreneur, but I was still a novice financial advisor. What I had *not* done was help people invest their wealth.

In my first nine years, I learned a great deal about the business by seeing firsthand how *not* to do things. Fortuitously, over the next nine years, Bud Jordan taught me what *to* do. What I found was I learned much more from the latter than I ever did from the former. Learning what not to do is a fool's errand. I spent the first nine years of my career learning the wrong way to build a business, suffered for it, and barely escaped bankruptcy. Over the next nine years, under Bud's tutelage, I learned what *to* do. The results were self-evident—my career and income exploded.

I was fortunate. Over those nine years prior to transitioning TCFin into a full financial services firm, I had been mentored by one of the best in the field. Bud and his team were masters of the trade, and I had a front-row seat.

While there are probably a million ways to do things wrong, there are only a few ways to do them right.

"While there are probably a million ways to do things wrong, there are only a few ways to do them right."

I Want to Be *That* Guy!

After leaving the *Top of the Table* meeting, the idea of not being *that guy* remained front of mind. Of course, I still had a business to run, yet the thought was never far away. Later that year, I attended a meeting in Vancouver, BC, Canada, the home of Clay Gillespie, the moderator of the session in San Francisco. Clay had succeeded Jim Rogers in their business, and I was keen on speaking to both about their transition.

It was great to hear the perspective of a successful buyer and a successful seller. What was interesting was how both agreed on one particularly important common theme—once Clay took over, Jim stepped away from managing the firm. Jim was not one to loiter about the office. He avoided offering well-intended, unsolicited advice. He allowed Clay to run the business, and Jim, although always available for solicited advice, pursued other passions. Even though the firm still bears Jim Rogers' name, he is ostensibly no longer involved in the business.

What is especially interesting is the company is stronger now than when it was sold—larger, better capitalized, and more profitable than ever! After speaking with them, it was evident the sale was a win for everyone. The clients were assured they would be looked after into their later lives. Consequently, it was a win for the clients. More employment opportunities emerged, which was a win for the staff. The partners of the firm won because they knew there was great value in their shares, making them want to stay and grow the firm. Clay won by being granted an opportunity he would otherwise never enjoy. Finally, it was a win for the founder, as he was able to transition into his next stage of life without the responsibility of caring for the firm and stepped into the financial freedom he always assured his customers they would receive.

Unbeknownst to Jim Rogers, he became the man who made me say, I want to be *that* guy! With the notable exception of his golf game, of course.

God's Money

Over the years, I met many people interested in buying our *book* of business, but few interested in the firm itself. The goal was to find a successor who was a good fit for our clients, staff, and our unique client value proposition. This would be no small accomplishment, as our firm was built on the unique premise of advising people from a Biblical worldview.

Since our earliest beginnings, I wanted a firm devoted to meeting the financial needs of Christian believers. In the early 1990s, we received a huge break. The manager of a local Christian radio station asked if I would consider a live on-air spot with the morning and afternoon DJ.

Christian radio has a concentrated and loyal audience of devout believers. The goal was to give the listeners solid financial advice from a Biblical standpoint. For over 25 years, with the help of the station's numerous on-air personalities, the show we called *God's Money* built an amazing following. Instead of advertising the company, the DJ and I would simply discuss financial questions and issues posted by listeners and answer them from a Biblical perspective rather than the secular viewpoint listeners might hear elsewhere.

Even though most of the listeners did not have sufficient assets for us to manage their accounts, the program helped TCFin gain instant credibility among our target audience—Christian believers. Consequently, about 90% of our clients came either directly or indirectly from *God's Money*. Our clients have an expectation of receiving advice from a devout believer with a Biblical worldview. Our clients fully expected any succession plan would continue this tradition, which significantly limited the field of potential candidates. While this might sound trite to some, it was, and still is, a big deal to both my clients and me. Whenever we broached the subject of succession or retirement with our clients, they would almost universally ask the same question: "Will your successor continue to advise us from a Biblical point of view?"

Providence Strikes Again

Not only did our successor need to be willing to keep the firm intact and be committed to continue our corporate philosophy, but I also wanted someone I could trust would continue to employ our existing staff. If a deal was not exceptional for them, I was committed to calling the whole thing off.

Eventually, I met a guy who knew a guy. Chad Justice was an ambitious young man who, after graduating from Baylor University in Waco, Texas, purchased a financial advisor's business in Orlando, about two hours north of our office. After several years, Chad expanded his company by buying an advisory firm in Gainesville (home of the University of Florida), and a third book of business from an advisor in Melbourne. Chad purchased both the Orlando and Gainesville operations with the intent of continuing them as business entities. In Melbourne, he bought the book of a small producer with the intent of merging his clients into the other two operations.

It is rare, even among Christian believers, for a firm to hold itself out as we have. To advise from a Biblical worldview takes special training most people have never considered, much less attained. Even though Chad never held his Orlando or Gainesville office out as a firm specializing in providing

Biblical financial advice to the Christian community, he totally embraced the idea. Furthermore, he was not looking to be involved in the day-to-day operation of our branch. He was looking for viable operations around the state of Florida that would continue and become part of and grow his company's brand. His vision was to keep the firm intact and replace the departing advisor with a competent replacement, with as little disruption to the business as possible. The new advisor would continue to work with the firm's clients long after the original advisor was gone. Since every book of clients is different, Chad knew it was incumbent upon him to find an advisor who understood the unique needs of the departing advisor's clientele. In the case of TCFin, Chad's model did not work without two key people—Mags and my long-time right-hand person, Kathy Walsh. Since Mags and Kathy were a known entity to the clients, Chad could not foresee purchasing the company without them! Last, but far from least, Chad is a devout believer who was excited to see our corporate culture continue.

Nevertheless, there was a rather large hindrance buffeting our negotiations: We did not share the same broker/dealer. Independent financial firms that offer products like mutual funds, direct investments, insurance products and the like, as well as those that charge commissions on securities trades, must be affiliated with the same broker/dealer (B/D). Those firms offering fee-based advisory services must also be affiliated with a common registered investment advisory (RIA) firm.

The advisors associated with TCFin, as well as the advisors associated with Chad, offer their services via brokerage (commission-based), and via advisory (fee-based). However, we did not share a common B/D or RIA, meaning unless one of us was willing to change affiliations, the two firms could not merge.

Changing a broker/dealer and/or RIA is a challenging, time-consuming, account by account process. It is not pleasant for the advisor nor client alike. After careful consideration of Chad's offer, I passed. We had no interest in changing our B/D and RIA affiliation simultaneously. Thereafter, we began to limit the focus to either someone already within our B/D or someone willing to move to our B/D and RIA rather than the other way around. The deal with Chad was as good as dead … until providence entered the picture.

As I expressed earlier, I am a big believer in providence—everything happens for a reason. I started my career as a life insurance agent for a reason. I became a sales manager for a reason. I failed in business, not once, but twice, for a reason. I worked for two major investment houses for a reason. With the assistance of some amazing people, we built an exceptional business for a reason. Everything happens for a reason.

The Calvinist may call it predestination and the skeptic, fate. I call it providence.

In 2017, the rumor mill was afire about the potential sale of our B/D and RIA to parties unnamed. Our B/D and RIA were owned by a British multi-national conglomerate with total assets of nearly a trillion pounds. Our B/D and RIA was a drop in the bucket compared to the assets of their parent. Once the decision was

> *"The Calvinist may call it predestination and the skeptic, fate. I call it providence."*

made to divest, our B/D and RIA, as you might have already guessed, was sold to Chad's B/D … Providence.

The Best of Both Worlds

By the later part of 2017, the B/D and RIA merger was finalized. All our accounts moved directly to the new B/D and RIA. There is no simpler way to change affiliations than via the merger of one firm into another. Within days of the announcement, Chad and I were in touch, and a plan was being formulated. We jointly determined our best course of action was to merge our firm with his.

A merger required a multi-step approach.

First, both Chad and I are registered principals, meaning one of us had to step down. This was easy. Placing the advisors supervised by me, as well as myself, under Chad's supervision was a logical decision.

Initially, no money changed hands between Chad and me. Our reps and I went under Chad's supervision, and we maintained our payouts at the same levels. A strange thing happened when Chad took over the supervisory duties. I liked it … a lot! My focus shifted from the supervision of reps to strictly managing accounts. Having been in a supervisory position for nearly 30 years, when Chad took it over, I suddenly realized how little it meant to me. In fact, I am not sure I ever enjoyed it as much as *endured* it. Although it took a few months to transition completely, by mid-2018, the merger was complete. All of our clients were advised of the merger, as well as our plan to ultimately turn over the reins to Chad and Mags.

Despite the uneven markets at the end of 2018, our profitability had never been better. Our clients and staff were happy. I was happy. Everything was going great. In fact, I started wondering why I had not done this a long time ago! In the meantime, Chad and I signed a Letter of Intent that spelled out all the particulars of the proposed buyout. This was a critical piece. The LOI identified the formula of valuing the company, the terms of separation, and what everyone could expect. However, the one thing the LOI did not identify was when the purchase would occur.

Amid all this change, suddenly, the business was fun again. I began thinking I could ride this wave for quite a while! As is the case with most sales of companies, the value of a company is calculated using a formula based on either a multiple of earnings, recurring revenue, or some combination of both. Since our earnings and recurring revenues were escalating, I began thinking if we continued to significantly increase earnings and recurring revenue, the value of the company in a few years would grow right along with it. From my perspective, this was the best of all worlds. On one hand, increased revenue and earnings are always good in the near term. On the other hand, higher revenues and earnings also increase valuation. As a result, the amount I would receive when we did pull the trigger on the purchase would be significantly more than if we decided to do it immediately. To say I was excited by the prospect of increased earnings now and reaping a larger reward in the future was an understatement!

Then, three important events, having nothing to do with the business, occurred that changed everything.

How Much Is Enough?

For many years, I have led a men's group that meets every Friday morning. We typically study a book applicable to issues facing men. Each week, we read a chapter, and every Friday morning, before we head off to work, we discuss the chapter of the book together. These guys have become like brothers to me. Over the years, the books we have read have made a stunning impact in our collective lives.

One week, as part of my preparation for facilitating our discussion, I ended up reading a parable about the importance of guarding against greed. The story starts out, "Beware and be on guard against every form of greed. For even when one has an abundance, his life does not consist of his possessions."[4] He goes on to tell the story of a farmer who had this outstanding piece of land yielding an abundant harvest. The farmer thinks to himself, "What am I going to do since I have no place to store my crops? This is what I will do: I will tear down my barns and build larger ones, and there I will store all my grain and my goods. And I will say to my soul, 'Soul, you have goods laid up for years to come. Take your ease. Eat, drink and be merry.'" But God says to him, "You fool! This night your soul will be required of you; who will own what you prepared for yourself?" The parable ends, "So is the man who lays up treasure for himself and is not rich toward God."[5]

In another text, Jesus is quoted as saying, "For what does it profit a man to gain the whole world and forfeit his own soul?"[6]

As I was preparing my thoughts, I was struck by the words Jesus used. The story is Jesus' way of establishing His original point—*guard against every form of greed*. Why? Because greed puts your soul at risk. The Greek word translated soul in both quotes is *psyche*—a word the English language borrowed directly from Greek.[7] The Ancient Greeks had a fascination with *psyche*. It means "breath," or, more literally, "what makes you breathe."

I spent hours wondering why Jesus used *psyche*, in lieu of the countless other words He could have chosen. My conclusion was He wanted His audience to know greed puts your *psyche*, who you are at the deepest level, at risk. Your psyche is the seat of your beliefs. It is who we really are, not who we pretend to be.

These two quotes impacted my own psyche in an extraordinary way. I began asking myself a very pointed question, "How much is enough?" Robert and Edward Skidelsky, in their book, *How Much Is Enough? Money and the Good Life,* wrote, "Experience has taught us that materialism knows no natural bounds, that it will expand without end unless we consciously restrain it. Capitalism rests precisely on this endless expansion of wants. That is why, for all its success, it remains so unloved. It has given us wealth beyond measure but has taken away the chief benefit of wealth: the consciousness of having enough."[8]

I found myself profoundly caught up in a simple, yet almost impossible, question to answer.

"How much is my soul worth?"

For the most part, I have always tried to heed my own advice. I diligently funded my retirement accounts, learned to live without the burden of debt, and consciously lived on way less than I earned. When from time to time I lost sight of these goals, I would catch myself and get back on track. As a result, like the farmer in the story, our family has been blessed with an abundant

"How much is my soul worth?"

harvest. As I thought about staying around just to make the buy-out grander, I was overcome by this parable. Was I tearing down my barns and building bigger ones just to store up what I would most likely not need anyway?

Pondering Mortality

A second, more profound event had an even greater impact on my decision. After my Dad passed in 2016, my mother decided to sell her house and move to a residential living community. Our family grew up in Florida, but after my sister graduated from university, she and her husband migrated to Richmond, Virginia. When my sister was pregnant with her third child, she asked my mom if she could come to Virginia and help her after her daughter was born. It was the early 1990s, and once my parents went to Virginia, they never came back. Even though Mom had lived in Virginia for around 20 years, after Dad passed she wanted to return to Florida. However, after about a year, missing Virginia and wanting to be closer to my sister, she moved back to Richmond. My mom was insistent on calling my brothers, who also live in Florida, and me almost daily. I wish I could say I dutifully talked to my Mom every time she called, but I did not. I must have 100 voicemails still saved on my phone of my mother leaving messages, just checking in.

My single greatest regret in life is I never realized my mother was dying. After returning to Virginia, my mother was frequently getting sick with various maladies. She had a chronic bronchial obstruction that never seemed to get better. She would start off every conversation with a cough and then apologize for not being able to speak clearly. What I did not realize then, but I know now, was she had a unique form of chronic obstructive pulmonary disease caused not by smoking—my mother never smoked anything—but by refractory (non-reversible) asthma she had since childhood. This obstruction left her constantly struggling to catch her breath. Selfishly, I was too impertinent to empathize with her illness. This meant my sister was forced to deal with the challenges of my mother's condition, which drove a wedge through our relationship that is still not completely resolved.

In what seemed to me like an instant, and to my sister a lifetime, Mom was on her deathbed. On June 21, 2019, my mother died. Mom was the glue keeping her four children together. When she was gone, what hit me hardest was I did not pay closer attention to her limited mortality.

Unlike my father, who had numerous health issues, Mom was always the healthy one. Her death made me ponder my own mortality. How did I want to spend the last years of my life? We all know, no one says on their deathbed, "I wished I had spent more time in the office."

The Perfect Closure

People say things come in threes. The third event setting up the decision to sell the practice, after examining my spiritual motivation and my mother's death, may surprise you. It certainly surprised me!

I love to play golf, and I am, pure and simple, a golf *fan*. If you ask me what I am doing the first week of April each year, I can already tell you—I am watching the Masters in Augusta. Every two years, professional American male golfers contest a series of matches against the best European professional men in a competition called the Ryder Cup. Professional women likewise have a competition called the Solheim Cup.

In 1990, Karsten Solheim, who founded The Ping Golf Equipment Company, was the driving force behind the creation of the biennial professional golf match for professional women golfers. The Solheim Cup is contested by teams representing Europe and America replicating the format used by the men in the Ryder Cup. It is played over three days, and each team has 12 players. What I love most about both the Solheim and Ryder Cup is there is no money involved, just the pride of winning the Cup! These are two of my favorite events because it is pure sport at its finest!

In 2019, the Solheim Cup matches were contested September 13-15 in Perthshire, Scotland, at the renowned Gleneagles Centenary Course. The USA golfers were defending the Cup by virtue of their 16½-11½ victory over the Euros in 2017. Notwithstanding the victor, there had always been a clear winner prior to the completion of the last match ... that is, until 2019.

At the end of both the first and second day, the matches were a dead heat. To win the Cup, a team needs to gain at least a tie of 14 points if they hold the Cup from the previous event, or 14½ points if they are attempting to wrest the Cup from the other squad. After 11 of the 12 matches were completed on the 3rd day, the overall match stood 13½-13½. The last match remaining pitted Marina Alex of the United States, a Solheim Cup rookie, against Suzann Pettersen of Europe, a veteran of 10 straight Solheim Cup events. Since the Americans were defending the Cup, if the US rookie won or tied, the Americans would retain the Cup. On the other hand, for Europe to win, the European veteran would have to win her match outright to gain the necessary 14½ points.

Alex and Petersen arrived at the last green with their match tied. They both had an opportunity to win the Cup for their squad with a final holed putt. Alex putted first, and her attempt from about 10 feet slid by the hole on the right, setting the stage for a dramatic completion of the event. Petersen's putt from just under 10 feet would be winner take all and decide the Cup! Miss, and the matches would finish 14-14, meaning the Yanks would retain the Cup. Make, and the Euros would win the Cup 14½-13½. As she was preparing to make the putt, I flashed back to 1991, when Bernhard Langer was a member of the European Ryder Cup team. He had virtually the same opportunity at Kiawah Island and missed, costing the Europeans the Ryder Cup. Would history be kind or cruel to the Euros this day?

Suzann drew her club back and, even before the ball went in, she dropped her putter and raised her arms in victory. The Europeans had won the event! Within seconds she was mobbed by her team, and the celebration began! As I watched, I was struck by the fact she never retrieved either the ball or her putter, leaving both for her caddie to sort out. After several minutes, the television crew finally caught up to her, and she could hardly catch her breath from the excitement of it all. She then stunned the world when, after making the biggest putt in Solheim Cup history, she said, "This is it! This is the last you will see of me playing in the Solheim. I cannot express it any better. I mean, to hole the winning putt, for the [win]." When she was in the interview room a little later, she went on to say, "I think this is the perfect closure—the end for my Solheim career, and also a nice, 'The End' for my professional career. Yeah, this is it! I am completely done."

Wait a minute! Did I hear her right? Did she just win the biggest event in her life and leave at the very top of her game? I literally stood up and clapped in my living room. I am sure my wife and daughters thought I was nuts, but when Suzann walked off, I walked off with her.

The next morning, I called Chad and said, "Let's make it happen. How quickly can we get this done?"

He said, "I am ready anytime you are."

Three and a half months later, I opened the next chapter of my book of life. As much as I loved the business, I am even more excited about what comes next.

Sure, I could have stuck around a little longer and filled a few more barns with grain, but Suzann gave me the courage to say, "I have done enough. It is time to make a difference in other ways. This is the perfect closure."

CHAPTER 2

THE ALICE IN WONDERLAND SYNDROME

There is a saying in the insurance business, "Throw them against the wall and see who sticks." Not a pretty metaphor by any means, but the number of people who wash out of every part of the financial services industry is immense.

There are countless reasons people quit. Poor training, impatience, lack of early success, reluctance to call strangers, fear, uncertain markets, and running out of money all make the list. The reasons may appear endless, but failure does not happen until someone quits! While there is no "I" in *team,* there is an "I" in *quit,* and somewhere, early on, every successful businessperson decides, no matter what, they are not going to quit.

They make the calls they do not want to make. They ignore the fifty *no's,* confident a *yes* is on the horizon. They know, intuitively, *nothing happens until **somebody** sells **someone something**.* The most common trait of the businessmen (and women) who build a successful business is ungirded tenacity—quitting is not an option!

I've Got Nowhere Else to Go

In the classic film, *An Officer and a Gentleman*, Richard Gere plays an officer candidate attempting to graduate from Naval Aviation Officer Candidate School—the first step toward becoming a Naval aviator. Gere's character, Zach Mayo, is convinced he can fake his way through OCS. He treats the school as if it is a game he cannot lose. Louis Gossett Jr. portrays a no-nonsense drill instructor, Emil Foley, who sees through Mayo's charade and wants him out. Sergeant Foley does everything in his power to get Mayo to quit. One day Foley takes Mayo out in the yard with one intention—force Mayo to quit.

Foley makes Mayo do more push-ups, pull-ups, and sit-ups than is seemingly possible. No matter, Mayo refuses to quit. At the brink of physical exhaustion, Foley, while Mayo is doing crunches on a concrete slab, begins a conversation with Mayo as he fights through more pain than he has ever experienced.

> **Foley:** *Why would a slick little hustler like you want to sign up for this kind of abuse anyway?*
> **Mayo:** I want to fly jets, sir.
> **Foley:** *My grandmother wants to fly jets.*
> **Mayo:** I've wanted it since I was a kid.
> **Foley:** *We're not talking about flying, we're talking about character.*
> **Mayo:** I've changed, sir.
> **Foley:** *No, you just polished up your act a little more, I want your DOR (Drop on Request—resignation)!*
> **Mayo:** No, sir! I am not going to quit!

Over and over, Foley badgers Mayo to quit. Mayo refuses to give in. Finally, Foley says, "*Then you can forget it. You're out!*"

The sudden realization that Foley, who had the power to throw him out, was going to end his dream, breaks Mayo. With tears flowing from his face to the concrete below, Mayo finally screams out the unfiltered truth:

Don't you do it, sir! Don't do it.
I've got nowhere else to go!
I've got nothing else.

In every successful career, there comes a day, or maybe hundreds of separate days, when the candidate decides, *I am not going to quit!* He or she makes a volitional choice. No matter how much it hurts, no matter how many disappointments, regardless of how hard it is, they are not going to quit.

I relate to Mayo. I vividly remember people telling me, over and over…

You're not going to make it, White!
You're not good enough!
Why are you even bothering?
Quit, man! There is no shame in quitting!

Maybe for some, there is no shame in quitting, but not for me. *An Officer and a Gentleman* was released in 1982. I am so thankful I saw it when I did. I was beginning my career, and like Mayo, I had no place else to go. I had nothing else. Quitting was never an option!

Finish Strong!

Nevertheless, when quitting *is* an acceptable option, it can easily become the *fallback* position. Everyone who has ever run a marathon or other endurance race knows there is a point in the race when the pain is so immense, all you want is to stop the pain. It is then the words of Sergeant Emil Foley ring out, "We're not talking about flying, we're talking about character." This is when you find out, like Mayo, whether you have the character to finish strong!

Running a business is a massive marathon, not a sprint. Marathons are hard. Most people do not even enter, much less finish. Nevertheless, anything worth doing is hard. Being self-employed, regardless of the industry, is HARD! No matter how difficult things become, how many people turn you down, how few people accept your proposal—you keep on running! Wanting to quit is normal. No one likes pain. Many quit, but finishers want the prize! They finish strong, because quitting is yielding, in the words of Winston Churchill, "to the apparently overwhelming might of the enemy." It is, in a word, *yielding to fear*. It is not an acceptable option!

When Winston Churchill was prime minister of England, he was invited to speak at the commencement of his boyhood school of Harrow.

> *"Never give in. Never give in. Never, never, never, never–In nothing, great or small, large or petty–never give in. Except to convictions of honor and good sense, never yield to force. Never yield to the apparently overwhelming might of the enemy."*

He stood up before the assembled teenaged boys and said: "Never give in. Never give in. Never, never, never, never—In nothing, great or small, large or petty—never give in. Except to convictions of honor and good sense, never yield to force. Never yield to the apparently overwhelming might of the enemy."[1]

Eventually, great men and women *decide* to finish strong. Finishing is not rocket science. It is hard work and requires unique abilities, to be sure. Most of all, it demands striving and persevering until one day you hear someone say, "Congratulations! You have fought the good fight. You have finished the race. You refused to quit. Come now and receive the reward which the judge is handing out to the winners of the race."

Remember this Florida truism: When you are up to your necks in alligators, it is hard to remember the original intent was to clean the swamp.

"When you are up to your necks in alligators, it is hard to remember the original intent was to clean the swamp."

Stop worrying about the alligators and get on with the *actual* task at hand. If the thing keeping you from finishing strong is the alligators, forget the alligators! Start cleaning the swamp, because they pay us for swamp cleaning, not alligator wrestling.

Beginning with the End in Mind

Stephen Covey, in his classic book, *The Seven Habits of Highly Effective People,* wrote the second habit of highly effective people is to **"Begin with the end in mind."** About this critical habit, he wrote, "Although Habit #2 applies to many different circumstances and levels of life, the most fundamental application of beginning with the end in mind is to begin today with the image, picture, or paradigm of the end of your life as your frame of reference or the criterion by which everything else is examined. Each part of your life—today's behavior, tomorrow's behavior, next week's behavior, next month's behavior—can be examined in the context of the whole, of what really matters most to you."

Covey went on to say, "To begin with the end in mind means to start with a clear understanding of the destination. It means to know where you are going so that you better understand where you are now and so that the steps you take are always in the right direction. It is incredibly easy to get caught up in the activity trap, in the busyness of life, to work harder and harder at climbing the ladder of success only to discover it is leaning against the wrong wall."[2]

When I first read Dr. Covey's book, I realized I was caught in an activity trap and headed to nowhere. No matter how hard I worked, I was constantly spinning my wheels. My goal was not to *thrive*; it was to *survive*. This led to a constant state of restarting. I was working hard, but my ladder was leaning against the wrong wall. I spent my time fighting alligators while completely neglecting the swamp. The problem was … I was stuck. I was caught up in what I now call *the Alice in Wonderland Syndrome*.

The Alice in Wonderland Syndrome

I am sure you remember Alice. She was this little girl who fell down a rabbit hole and ended up in Wonderland. As she wanders about, trying to find her way through Wonderland, she happens upon the Cheshire Cat. Alice and the Cat engage in a conversation:

Alice: Would you tell me, please, which way I ought to go from here?
Cheshire Cat: *That depends a good deal on where you want to get to.*
Alice: I don't much care where—
Cheshire Cat: *Then it doesn't matter which way you go…*
Alice: So long as I get somewhere, Alice added as an explanation.
Cheshire Cat: *Oh, you're sure to do that, if you only walk long enough.*[3]

Most people are on their way to *Somewhere*, with little to no idea what or where Somewhere is … *but they are on their way there.* What the Cat is implying is: If you do not know where you are going, any road will take you there!

The primary reason people quit is, like Alice, *it does not matter which way they go, so long as they get to Somewhere.* With little idea of where they are going or why they are going there, these Alices meander through life without commitment, shifting from job to job, career to career. They enter marriages that are doomed before they start. They

> *"If you do not know where you are going, any road will take you there!"*

move incessantly from one place to another. Nothing is satisfying. Little is good enough. Then, one day, they are 67 years old, bagging food at the grocery store. The truth is, unless you know where Somewhere is, you are probably not going to stumble over it!

A friend of mine is a successful doctor. I asked him once, "Joe, what is the secret to your success?" He looked at me and said: "One spouse. One career. One home."

"I have one wife. I have one career. I have one place I call home," he told me. "Before I married my wife, I envisioned her, not as the beauty she was, but as the grandmother she would become. I fell in love with the grandmother she would become. Once I was sure she was the woman I wanted to be with when I was a grandpa and she was a grandma, I begged her to marry me!"

> *"One spouse. One career. One home."*

"Before I went to medical school," he continued, "I envisioned myself as a busy doctor turning my successful practice over to my successor. Once I could see myself finishing with a successful practice someone else was willing to buy, I enrolled in med school. Once I graduated and completed my internship, I thought about where I wanted to raise my children and live out my life. My wife and I fell in love with Stuart, Florida. We put down roots and never found a reason to leave. Was it easy? Not a chance—it was hard. I cannot tell you how many times I wanted to just throw in the towel and quit. But I knew quitting was not an option."

Joe began with the end in mind. He is now in his 70s. He sleeps beside that same woman he envisioned as his life partner, the grandmother he begged to marry when she was a young beauty! He sold his practice several years back to another internal medicine group, just as he envisioned. And, yes, he still lives in Stuart, Florida, in the same house he built for his family over 30 years ago. One spouse, one career, one home—what a concept!

It seems almost unimaginable, but Lewis Carroll's masterpiece, *Alice's Adventures in Wonderland*, known most simply as *Alice in Wonderland*, was originally published in 1865—the same year Abraham Lincoln was assassinated at Ford's Theatre. The story of Alice has been captivating readers throughout the years, and for good reason—we are more like Alice than we might expect. Some prepare for their career early and seize the day. Most fall down a rabbit hole into an unexpected adventure. Like Alice, they shrink themselves down to a size necessary to squeeze into their own form of Wonderland. Then, they run through Wonderland on their way to Somewhere as aimlessly as Alice ran through hers.

Alice was on her way to Somewhere without any idea where or what Somewhere was. One of the toughest days in life is to surmise you are on the road to Somewhere with little to no idea where Somewhere is, but you are on your way there. As I mentioned earlier, when you do not know where you are going, any road will take you there. Scarcity of direction is common for those lacking vision. In fact, an absence of vision has become the norm, while those *with* vivid vision are the exception.

If I could give one piece of advice to a young person, avoid the Alice in Wonderland Syndrome! Stop wandering around Wonderland on your way to Somewhere. Take Dr. Joe's advice—decide now what you want out of life by beginning with the end in mind and then go for it with ruthless conviction. If I were a newly minted entrepreneur, I would attempt to envision, as Dr. Joe did, what I want my life to look like at age 60, even though I might be less than halfway there. Can you envision yourself married to the same person you are with today? Can you see yourself as financially independent? Can you imagine, as Joe did, seeing yourself finishing with a successful practice someone else was willing to buy? Or is a life of beating off the alligators, instead of cleaning the swamp, impeding the way?

Be an Owner, Not a Renter

In *Seven Habits*, Covey speaks a great deal about making paradigm shifts. Dr. Covey taught us that a paradigm is the way you see, interpret, or understand the world. He was not talking about a visual sense of sight, but rather how you perceive, understand, or interpret the objective. Covey saw paradigms as if they were maps. "A map is not the territory itself," Covey wrote, "rather it is something that describes the territory and tells you how to maneuver within it. Too often people establish a paradigm—or better said, a belief system—that is just incorrect. Can you imagine trying to find your way around Chicago with a map of Detroit?"[4] To begin with the end in mind is understandably difficult, but it can be life-altering.

Here is a worthwhile paradigm shift: Be an owner, not a renter. I am not necessarily talking about real estate. I am talking about life. If you join an organization, be an owner, not a renter. Business owners are not renters of the business. Owners do not leave in the middle of the night. Renters do it all the time. Owners fix broken things. Renters call the owner. Owners are intentional about increasing the value of their property. Renters want low rent and could not care less about the value of the property. Owners are always improving their property, fighting to preserve it, and making it as beautiful as it can be. Renters ... not so much! Taking ownership is a key paradigm shift and the secret to being tenacious.

Early Endings

I began my career in Fort Lauderdale, Florida, when I was 21 years old. I started as an insurance agent, and at age 23, I was asked to recruit other agents. There was a problem. I had no idea what I was doing. In due time, they fired me. Suddenly, I was an unemployed twenty-something crashing down the proverbial rabbit hole. For a couple of years, I was waist-deep in the Alice in Wonderland Syndrome, wandering around in my own Wonderland where, like Alice, *it did not matter which way I went ... so long as I got to Somewhere.* Until, to my surprise, I saw an advertisement posted by E.F. Hutton & Company. The advertisement said Hutton was looking for experienced life insurance agents to sell insurance to the clients of their brokers.

When I met the recruiter, he asked me if I would have any objection to moving north. I assumed he meant New Jersey or something.

He chuckled and said, "No, Stuart."

"Stuart, where is Stuart?" I had never heard of the place.

"It's a great little town about 90 miles north of Fort Lauderdale with one of Hutton's best offices."

He arranged for the manager to see me that afternoon. Floyd D. Jordan, known by all as Bud, was branch manager and the largest producer in the branch. Little did I know, Bud Jordan would eradicate the Alice in Wonderland Syndrome from my life for good. Near the end of my interview, Bud said, "This is an investment firm. However, I do not need you to sell investments. I need you to sell insurance. It is all you do. Can you do that?"

"Yes, sir."

"Fine. Now, remember I told you this," he said. "Always do what is in the best interest of the person sitting in front of you, and your interest will always take care of itself."

> *"Always do what is in the best interest of the person sitting in front of you, and your interest will always take care of itself."*

This was my first experience understanding the importance of Covey's second habit, *beginning with the end in mind*. From the beginning, I knew exactly where I was going. The goal was simple. Be the absolute best insurance producer for E.F. Hutton and its clients possible. I also knew what *Somewhere* was not. It was not selling investments and engaging in activity that did not lead to my becoming the absolute best insurance producer for E.F. Hutton and their clients.

We negotiated a salary, shook hands, and he said he would see me bright and early the next morning. I was on cloud nine! I woke up not knowing where Stuart, Florida, was. The next day I was going to be working there.

90 Miles North and 90 Miles South

As I started the car, panic hit me like a ton of bricks. It suddenly dawned on me I never talked to my wife. She had no idea I went to Stuart to interview for a job. Had I lost my mind? How do you take a position without ever mentioning you are interviewing for it to your wife? I was dead, and I knew it.

When I arrived home, my wife, Grace, met me with a scowl. "Where were you today?" In a matter of seconds, the phenomenal script I had formulated on my 90-minute ride home was out the window and I was stumbling and bumbling to explain what had happened. When I got to the part about accepting a job in Stuart, she looked at me dead in the eyes and screamed, "STUART?! You took a job in Stuart?" Unlike me, she knew exactly where Stuart was and said flatly, "Well, I hope you enjoy driving to Stuart every day. There is no way I will ever move to Stuart, Florida. I hope you enjoy the drive."

The next morning, I rose early and was on the road before the sun even considered coming up. The car was quiet. The day before, as I was formulating my failed script, I silenced the radio as I began my journey home. With all the communication options available in cars today, automotive communication technology in the 1980s was primitive. The range on AM and FM bands was barely 20 or 30 miles from the tower. Fortunately, my little Honda had a cassette tape player, and I had 90 miles in each direction to use the time wisely! Over the years, I had accumulated quite a collection of cassettes from all sorts of speakers, and now I had the opportunity to listen to these tapes uninterrupted every day, driving 90 miles north and 90 miles south.

It Is All About Trust

Even if you know everything there is to know about the problems people might have and how to solve them, you still need the opportunity to share those ideas with someone. As such, I needed the trust of the brokers in the office, or this would be a short-lived experiment because *nothing happens until somebody sells someone something.*

About a week into my tenure, Bud took the entire office—brokers, management, staff, you name it—out to lunch. I always wore a suit and tie in the office, but on this day, I left my coat in the car. Bud came to my office and asked if I wanted to go to lunch with "the gang." Even though I did not know where we were going or what to expect, I eagerly said yes and got into Bud's car feeling like I had just gotten picked for the cool kid's team.

At lunch, I really felt like a part of the group. When we were finishing up, I mentioned to Bud I needed to use the restroom and would be right back. I swear I was gone less than three minutes. When I returned, everyone was gone! The waitress said Bud told her I would handle the bill. Determined to keep my composure, I reached for my wallet only to realize it was in my coat in my car. I went to Jake, the owner, and explained to him my credit card was in my car and I would be right back. I went down to retrieve my coat and remembered I did not have a car—I came with Bud. I walked back to the office, drove back to Jake's, and paid the bill for a 50-person lunch with money I did not have. When I returned to the office, I was greeted with a standing ovation. This was my early initiation, and I had passed. I was now the newest member of this unique fraternity Bud called *the gang*.

Soon I was meeting with clients and writing more insurance than I ever dreamed imaginable. At year-end, I was the leading life specialist in the country for E. F. Hutton and was asked to speak at the annual conference in Dallas alongside Roger Staubach, the Hall of Fame quarterback of the Dallas Cowboys. Life was suddenly amazing in ways I had never even dreamed possible just a year earlier!

Doors Close, Windows Open

In October 1987, two significant events occurred. First, the stock market crashed. On what became known as Black Monday, the Dow Jones

Industrial Average was down over 22%. It was the largest one-day percentage drop of the Dow in history, eclipsing Black Tuesday, the worst one-day percentage collapse of the market during the crash of 1929 that launched *The Great Depression.*[5]

Black Monday—the correction of the 19th of October 1987—significantly impacted not only *the* world, but *my* world. E.F. Hutton & Company collapsed. A few months later, Hutton was absorbed into Shearson Lehman, never to exist again. While Shearson offered positions to every Hutton account executive, they eliminated the insurance specialist program! We had just moved to Stuart, and I was going to be out of a job.

It was then I began to understand the need to *end with the beginning in mind,* the inverse of the precept Dr. Covey taught. When word came that Shearson was eliminating the insurance specialist program, Bud came to me and said he was working on it. Even though my short tenure with Hutton was ending, there was an even better beginning that I never saw coming.

A week or so later, Bud asked me to join him on a conference call with the CEO of Prudential-Bache Securities. Unbeknownst to me, Bud was negotiating to bring the entire office from Hutton to Bache. The CEO asked Bud and me to spearhead a pilot insurance program for Bache in Florida, replicating what we had at Hutton.

In February 1988, just four months post-Black Monday, we joined Prudential-Bache and started TCFin soon after. For seven years, TCFin was the exclusive insurance distribution agency for Prudential-Bache Securities in the state of Florida. This opportunity was even better than what we had at Hutton.

Our agreement with Prudential-Bache allowed our company, TCFin, to contract with various insurance carriers and provide cutting-edge insurance solutions and products to Bache brokers in Florida. We were quite a team, and I loved every minute … until I did not.

After nine years, I lost my appetite for the politics of working in a wirehouse. It was also obvious Bache was preparing to rein us in and bring the operation in-house. I went to Bud and said I wanted to leave Bache to start an independent insurance and investment firm. Providentially, I had met the COO and CMO of an independent broker-dealer on a scuba diving trip. They invited me to join their independent broker-dealer, and I never looked back.

Every ending is an opportunity to begin anew. It happened when I left Fort Lauderdale and began afresh in Stuart at E.F. Hutton & Company. After

> *"Every ending is an opportunity to begin anew."*

the door at Hutton closed, it led to a window opening at Bache. After Bache ended, another window opened as an independent advisor. The merger and ultimate sale of my company began the next chapter in my life. These were all endings that led to even better new beginnings.

Building a Company Worth Buying

Notwithstanding, the best businesses are the ones people want to buy. However, even the best businesses can slip into the Alice in Wonderland Syndrome. The best way to keep the business from slipping is to stay intentional.

Salable businesses are intentional about keeping accurate books and records, finding the right clients to serve, and products to sell. The most salable businesses are self-managing companies with competent staff and associates that are generating significant recurring revenue. They make sure the loss of the founder or some other key person will not decimate the firm. Most of all, businesses worth buying are never dependent upon one person.

They are intentional about team building and allowing people to demonstrate their unique abilities.

Finally, salable businesses find ways to intentionally create recurring revenue in the business. Recurring revenue models are attractive to buyers. Unfortunately, in many cases, recurring revenue means less immediate income now. The greatest inhibitor of moving a business from a transaction-based revenue model to a recurring revenue model is the need for the *immediate* income transactions produce. When a firm needs to make payroll and pay overhead, it needs revenue sources that provide the necessary funds to stay afloat. It is hard to earn enough to pay the bills while concurrently building recurring revenue. It takes time some firms may not have if they do not generate enough to stay in business.

Finding sources of revenue that keep the business afloat while building secondary sources of recurring revenue can be challenging. In our firm, we mixed commission-based products, which tend to pay up-front commissions to provide adequate funds to pay the bills. Advisory business was our best source of recurring revenue. We were intentional about adding advisory business on an ongoing basis. The more advisory business we added, the more attractive the firm was to a buyer. The same is true in every industry. Recurring revenue provides the best source of predictable income and ultimately increases the value to a successor.

As a business owner, keep two things in mind. First, do not create recurring revenue at the expense of the client. If a firm takes care of the client first, the needs of the firm will take care of themselves. Second, pay close attention to the firm's P&L. Know precisely what the company earns and where it goes.

Even if your business has been around for 30 years, look for ways to intentionally make the company more marketable. The more a founder structures the business to be sold one day, the better the results will be for the founder, both near and long term. For many entrepreneurs, especially early on, it is hard to envision their business being much more than a fine way to conduct business and maximize income. As the company grows, it becomes easier to imagine the business having residual value. When you intentionally build a marketable firm, down the road, someone will be begging you to sell it to them.

Always End with the Beginning in Mind!

This is the name of the book for a reason. Life is about managing endings. When you end with the beginning in mind, endings are not *the end*. Endings are new beginnings—for founders as well as successors. Be intentional about ending on your terms!

Life is just a series of endings and new beginnings. This is a foreign concept to many entrepreneurs who think they are supposed to hang in there forever. The movie ends. The television show ends. This book ends. No matter how pleasant or difficult the weekend was, you get up on Monday morning and get back to work. Do not worry about endings. They are a natural course of events. Rather, embrace them.

The biggest reason most entrepreneurs become entrepreneurs in the first place is they have a staunch belief running their own company is better for their clients, staff, associates, and everyone else connected to the firm. Of course, they also believe owning their own organization will be better, both in the near and long term, for themselves. Entrepreneurs relish the freedom to establish the culture of their own firm. By the same token, freedom can be their greatest risk. When a business owner is intentional about building a business that is marketable, they can build a great organization. They can mitigate risk and have a firm that is great for their clients and associates long after the founder has handed the reins to someone else.

CHAPTER 3

SUCCESSION OR CESSATION, THE CHOICE IS YOURS

W e have all seen the idyllic posters with these types of retirement quotes:

"Retirement: When you stop lying about your age and start lying around the house."

Is this really the goal of highly effective people—to lie around all day and do nothing? Let's debunk a myth here, right off the bat. It is incongruent to equate retirement to succession. While retirement and succession are not mutually exclusive, there are not many who can go from full blast to full stop. In my experience, successful people find their significance in their work. It is often what brings, for better or worse, *purpose* to their lives. That does not frequently change when someone turns some arbitrary age.

"Note: For purposes of this book, succession is defined as the act or process of one thing coming after another thing with the intent of continuing that thing. Cessation is defined as the act or process of bringing something to an end."

As we said in the last chapter, this book is entitled *Always End with the Beginning in Mind* for a reason. Life is a series of endings with concurrent new beginnings. It is about discovering why you exist and then *re*discovering why you continue to exist. I once heard Lou Holtz say, "The two most important days in life are the day you were born and the day you discovered why you were born." Some claim Mark Twain said it, and maybe he did, but I heard it from Coach Holtz. While the question of *why you were born* can be fluid, be certain of this: no one is born to lay around and become immersed in self-gratification.

In the late 1950s, folk singer Pete Seeger put music to a poem from the third chapter of the Book of Ecclesiastes in the Old Testament. Consequently, the song *Turn! Turn! Turn!* was born. Except for a small adjustment to add rhyme, the lyrics of the song are essentially what was written in the book of Ecclesiastes eons ago. The song was hardly known until 1965, when The Byrds tweaked Seeger's music a bit and released it as the title song on their second album. The song has become legendary, been covered countless times, and now resides in the Rock and Roll Hall of Fame. The original poem, as written in the book of Ecclesiastes, juxtaposes the contradictions of life; the endings and beginnings always playing in concert with one another.

To everything there is a season
And a time to every purpose, under heaven
A time to be born, a time to die
A time to plant, a time to reap
A time to kill, a time to heal
A time to laugh, a time to weep
A time to build up, a time to break down
A time to dance, a time to mourn
A time to cast away stones, a time to gather stones together
A time of love, a time of hate
A time of war, a time of peace
A time to embrace, a time to refrain from embracing

A time to gain, a time to lose
A time to rend, a time to sew
A time for love, a time for hate
A time for peace

To which Seeger added, "I swear it's not too late."[1]

The poem catches the realities of a lifetime. There is a season, a time for everything. The author might also have added *there is a time to begin, a time to end, and a time to begin again.*

Succession allows a person to consider a time to discover new significance outside a current business while simultaneously allowing others the opportunity to grow and reap where the original person has sown.

Succession most certainly does not mean doing nothing without worrying about getting caught!

Barring either a physical or mental incapacity, successful people are not cut out for lying around the house counting their retirement shekels. No one finds significance in self-gratification. Rather, true significance is found in self-sacrifice and contributing to the welfare of others. The notion of buying a villa, playing golf, euchre, or pickleball until you die of boredom is an enigma of the modern concept of retirement and simply does not work.

> *"Succession most certainly does not mean doing nothing without worrying about getting caught!"*

A Brief History of Retirement

The modern concept of retirement—or, more specifically, retiring at age 65—is a product of the Industrial Revolution of the 19th and early

20th century. It became entrenched in western lifestyle during the time when governments, beginning with Germany in 1883, made retirement pensions a part of public policy. The 19th century was not kind to the working class. People were made to work unbearably long hours. Child labor was common. Workers were often mistreated with verbal and physical abuse. Wages and benefits were a joke. Everything from degrading remarks to sexual harassment was systemic, not only allowed but *encouraged* by those in charge. Many employers purposely understaffed and routinely overworked and underpaid employees. Working conditions were, at best, ragged, and, at worst, deadly.

During this time, workers sought to unite. Labor parties, unions, socialist and communist groups sought to change the plight of the workers. One of the most vocal antagonists was Karl Marx, who, in 1847, wrote the Communist Manifesto. Marx believed society's history of class struggles, what he referred to as *the exploitation by the bourgeoisie*[2] *of the proletarians*[3], was "disintegrating civilization [and creating] retrograde classes throughout the industrial world."[4]

What is intriguing is modern retirement finds its roots in Marxism. Karl Marx made it a key part of his *post-revolution plan.*[5] David Warsh, in his book, *Knowledge and the Wealth of the Nations*, writes when Marx was asked what life would be like after the revolution, he stated, "The division of labor would all but disappear. A man might fish in the morning, hunt in the afternoon, rear cattle in the evening, and philosophize after dinner, just as he desires, without ever becoming a fisherman, hunter, shepherd or critic."[6]

In an attempt to preempt the growing Communist movement in Germany, around the time of Marx's death, German Chancellor Otto "the Ironfist" Von Bismarck, a staunch conservative, announced that anyone over the age of 65 would be forced to retire, and the German government would pay them a pension for life. Marx died in 1883 at the age of 64—the very year Bismarck introduced the German version of "pensions for the elderly." Marx's influence was immense when he died. Indeed, his philosophies were taking hold all over the world in the late 19th century. Bismarck was not trying to promote retirement planning. This was strictly political expedience.[7]

The average male died before age 60 in the 1880s. As such, a 65-year-old was like an 80-year-old today. In his attempt to assuage the left, he presumed forcing people to retire and paying them a monthly stipend for the rest of their short lives would get the socialists and communists off his back. Also, it would not cost much—hardly anyone lived that long, anyway! The United States embraced the philosophy when it introduced Social Security in 1935, using the same age of 65 for similar reasons as Bismarck.

Throughout most of history, people worked until they either died or became infirm. Because people, by today's standards, died young, there was no need to even consider pensions. Then penicillin came along, and life expectancy exploded!

A Lesson from the Golden Bear

An excellent example of how to view succession planning is found with Jack Nicklaus. Nicklaus is arguably the best golfer of all time. Many of his records in golf may never be broken. More importantly, his influence on golf is unprecedented among athletes of *any* sport in *any* era. He is not only one of the greatest golfers of all time, but one of the most prolific golf course designers. By the time he was in his late 40s, even though he was still playing golf competitively, he focused much of his time on building golf courses. He built his 200th course before age 60, and Nicklaus and his company are responsible for over 400 courses (and still counting) worldwide! Mr. Nicklaus' last competitive round of golf was at the British Open at age 65 in 2005, the same year he received the highest award Congress can bestow—the Congressional Gold Medal. At the time, he said, "Most people work all their life to retire to play golf. I played golf to retire to work."[8]

> *"Most people work all their life to retire to play golf. I played golf to retire to work."*

Mr. Nicklaus' work ethic is legendary. However, if you study his business record, there are some struggles along with his many successes. I met Mr. Nicklaus in 1999, when one of my clients, an employee of The Nicklaus Group, died in a plane crash. Things were rough for the Golden Bear Companies in the latter part of the 1990s. Even though the company was bleeding money, and some thought it might not even survive, Mr. Nicklaus put his employee's family ahead of his corporate challenges. He provided significant financial assistance to his employee's wife and children as they tried to recover from their tragic loss.

I saw firsthand the secret of Jack's unprecedented success. It traces back to the way he looks out for the interests of other people. Mr. Nicklaus did not have to do what he did for this family. While under absolutely no obligation, he put people over profit.

His ability to raise up the right people and pass on leadership at the proper time borders on mythical. His companies sell everything from fine wine, to ice cream and lemonade, to golf equipment and clothing lines galore. In 2007, he sold a half interest in The Nicklaus Companies to billionaire-entrepreneur Howard Milstein. His son, Jackie, has been overseeing the golf course design business for years now, and, in 2018, he stepped away completely from all his enterprise work to focus on growing the Nicklaus Children's Health Care Foundation. In 2004, Jack started his charitable foundation and raised nearly $100 million in his spare time! He is now well on the way to raising an additional $100 million for the foundation before his 85th birthday.

Here's the $64,000 question: Has Jack Nicklaus retired? Jack was asked this question in a recent interview with Tom D'Angelo of the Palm Beach Post. He smiled and replied, "[Retire] from *what?*" He went on to say, "I do not think I really am going to retire. I still [have] a lot of things to do."[9]

Mr. Nicklaus is a picture of what post-modern retirement can look like—assuming one remains healthy. Jack has never been foolish enough to think he can beat back the hands of time. He is keenly aware anyone's health can turn against them suddenly, as it did for his good friend, Arnold Palmer. Any business can outlive its founder with the Jack Nicklaus approach.

A proper succession plan does not necessarily ask you to retire. It does, however, require you to have confidence in the people selected to succeed the founder and the processes implemented over time. A workable succession plan requires leaving the day-to-day operation of *your baby* to others. Proper succession gives an organization the opportunity to be reborn. Always ending with the beginning in mind is more than just a turn of phrase. It is what allows an organization, and its founder, the opportunity to open their next chapter in their book of life.

> *"Always ending with the beginning in mind is more than just a turn of phrase. It is what allows an organization, and its founder, the opportunity to open their next chapter in their book of life."*

While not many of us are ready to walk off at the height of our career, as Suzanne Pedersen did when she won the Solheim Cup for Europe, many people fear transitioning their business to someone else. I contend that the fear of succession is a matter of identity. Many folks cannot see themselves in another capacity and find it hard to let go. The business is who they *are*. They have seen modern retirement, and they want no part of it. Without something to continue to stir the juices, many will leave only when they are left with no other choice. The idea of leaving before they *must* exit is an enigma they refuse to face.

However, this is not about retirement. It is about succession, and the two are vastly different.

The Implications of Exiting Late

Few businesspeople appreciate the implications of exiting late. The longer you wait, the more it concerns clients. No one is indispensable. It is a fallacy of ego. If you genuinely care about clients, arrange for someone else to help them for the long haul. Transitioning before you *need* to transition can grow client retention exponentially and increase the ultimate value to a buyer.

Think from an investor's point of view. Older people typically have older clients. Assuming equal billings, a 60-year old client has more residual value to an investor than a 70-year-old. Even though they are 10 years apart in age, the difference between working with a client for 15 years rather than 25 years (assuming equal mortality) is a 60% increase in potential revenue.[10]

Further, most 70-year-old clients are growing more fiscally conservative, spending less and drawing down their accumulated resources. Conversely, their 60-year-old counterpart is earning, saving, and spending more. Suppose one organization serves strictly retirees while another serves primarily pre-retirees. All things being equal, the latter is more valuable to an investor than the former. That said, the longer an owner waits to sell or be succeeded, unless they significantly change their client mix, the less valuable the business will become. In my experience, waiting too long diminishes value to the point many people never transition, and the business goes to the grave with them.

Irrespective of the reason, waiting too long not only reduces the opportunity to sell, but the founder misses the enjoyment they might experience in a new challenge. When it comes to exiting, it will either be at your volition, someone else's volition, or God's volition. While we cannot know when, where, how, or even why, everyone knows *to whom* this certainty applies. There is only one thing guaranteed in life—eventually, everything ends.

One of the great curiosities of life is while folks are quick to give lip service to their ultimate mortality, few have done much to secure a future beyond themselves. As a starting point, the very least every practitioner should do is establish a contingency plan should they die or become disabled. Nevertheless, the sheer lack of preparation to exit shows how little people really believe *it* can happen to them. Out loud, they say, "Yeah, that could happen," while unwittingly thinking, *But not to me ... at least not for a long time.*

> *"There is only one thing guaranteed in life—eventually, everything ends."*

Why not avoid an exit being an *event*? What if it was just a smooth closing of one chapter and the opening of another? When you give exiting the attention it deserves, everyone wins. Failing to pay attention can be disastrous for those you leave behind.

She Did Not Plan to Fail ... She Just Failed to Plan

Liz (a pseudonym) was a terrific financial advisor. At 68 years of age, she was still going strong. South Florida is one of the most affluent areas in the world. It was Liz's domain, and the perfect environment for her to excel. She was a fit, active gym-rat, and the picture of good health. A solo practitioner and tireless worker, she became one of the top producers at her

B/D. She had a solid book of affluent clients. They loved her and the work she did on their behalf. She had a strong recurring stream of income. While we were not friends, everyone knew Liz. Her reputation was impeccable. Colleagues looked up to her, and her staff had been with her for years.

In financial services organizations, there are typically four essential roles of those in the firm. There are what Clay Gillespie calls *Finders, Minders, Grinders,* and what I call the Director of First Impressions. As the title suggests, Finders find clients. Minders oversee the client accounts. Grinders are responsible for everything administrative. Finally, every good office has a person who makes the experience of calling the company, meeting with an advisor, and every other social aspect of the firm, pleasant—the Director of First Impressions—because you can never make a *first* impression again.

While, especially in solo practices, these tasks often overlap, no business can exist without clients. As we said previously, n*othing happens until somebody sells someone something.* While somebody needs to mind the store, and somebody needs to handle paperwork and the client experience, every business needs Finders. Somebody needs to put cheeks in the seats.

> *"Somebody needs to put cheeks in the seats."*

As with most solo practitioners, Liz was an amazing Finder. However, she an equally good Minder. She not only found virtually every client of the firm, but she looked after their affairs and made sure the staff (the Grinders) carried out her wishes, precisely. She set the stage, and her staff kept everyone smiling.

Over the years, I have met thousands of financial advisors, insurance agents, lawyers, accountants, and others in small business. With few exceptions, in a small company, the client's relationship is primarily connected to their individual point of contact, rather than to the firm. Clients are looking for someone they can trust. Especially in a small retail operation, clients are looking for someone to guide them. As such, one consistent trait of successful entrepreneurs is their ability to create an emotional connection with their clients. The best operators have the gift of knowing how to build a strong connection with their clients, and, by extension, build an equally strong connection to the firm.

In financial businesses, as folks navigate the myriad of financial decisions they face in their lives, having someone they absolutely trust is a primary differentiator between successful practices and those merely eking out a living. Successful advisors have an emotional attachment with their clients that makes their work more a calling than a career. Liz checked all the boxes.

Then *it* happened. Liz was diagnosed with Stage IV pancreatic cancer. Six weeks later, she was gone. Everyone associated with her—her clients, her staff, and her B/D had to face the stark reality of life without Liz. Tragically, Liz was not granted the gift of time. Had she lived for months or even years after her diagnosis, she might have had time to find and introduce her successor. Unfortunately, a six-week terminal diagnosis is analogous to being hit by a bus. You never see it coming, and there is nothing anyone can do to stop its outcome.

Everyone, whether they know it or not, has established an exit plan for their business. Some have established a *succession* plan. Most have a *cessation* plan. Too often, gifted entrepreneurs build practices not to *succeed* (the root of succession), but to *cease* (the root of cessation) after they exit.

I want you to ask yourself two questions, right here, right now.

What would happen to my business if I were Liz?
If I had six weeks to live, would my business succeed,
or would it eventually cease?

The Best Interest of the Person in Front of You

David Grau, the founder of FP Transitions, a firm specializing in helping financial advisors create sustainable practices, wrote, "As an industry we have a problem to solve: 99 percent of today's independent financial services and advisory practices will not survive their founder's retirement or the end of the founder's individual career. When the advisor leaves, for any reason, it is over. And that [must] change. Clients have a clear expectation of advice tailored to the length of their lives, not to the length of their advisor's career."[11]

As I said earlier, Bud Jordan was my primary mentor. Bud never operated an independent advisory practice. He spent his entire career in a wirehouse. He certainly had the skill, the wherewithal, and the financial resources to pull off an independent operation. However, by the time independence had taken a significant foothold, he was too entrenched in the wirehouse ethos to leave. He also believes affluent clients trust a wirehouse to provide advice should their advisor exit the business or the firm.

"Clients have an expectation their world will not be overly impacted," he once told me, "if their advisor retires, gets sick, hurt, or dies. They have faint interest in having to deal with a different firm if I am suddenly not around." Like Grau writes, in Bud's experience, he has rarely seen independent firms survive either a founder's retirement or death.

Furthermore, in his experience, wealthy, especially the elderly, clients are highly resistant to change. Bud frequently said it is not his job to get people to change their minds. His job is to understand what clients believe rather than attempt to convert their thinking. Keep in mind, it was Bud who told me the secret to success was to, "Always do what is in the best interest of the person in front of you, and your interest will take care of itself."

In my world, this premise of always trying to look out for the best interest of others is inviolable. What I respect most about this statement is it does not suggest our interest is unimportant. Our interest is particularly important. Furthermore, our interest is *achieved* when the needs of others are put first.

A great succession plan puts the needs of the firm, clients, staff, vendors, B/D, and successors above the needs of the proprietor. I am not completely sure why, but, when you unselfishly look out for the interest of others, you are blessed. I cannot quantify this mystery scientifically, other than to tell you it ultimately becomes a win for everybody. Indeed, if you are

> *"If you are about to do something that is not a win for everyone involved, don't do it!"*

about to do something that is not a win for everyone involved, don't do it! I promise you will regret it.

However, all of this presupposes you have a firm and not a one-man band. Unfortunately, Liz was the entire band. When her music stopped, her cessation plan was implemented. Within days of her passing, the clients started to call to ascertain who was going to manage their affairs. In short order, her clients were also calling other advisors. I discovered this firsthand when I learned of her death after one of her clients made one of those calls to me. While she had a wonderful staff, they were not able to replace her. As is the case in every cessation plan, her clients began leaving like those on a sinking ship.

To her B/D's credit, a short time after she died, they recruited a nice young man to move into her office and attempt to salvage the business. While he did a yeoman's job of trying to keep as many clients as he could, the fallout was immense. Her family will never receive the value they would otherwise have enjoyed had she created a plan for her succession ahead of time. Without a named successor, her clients were left without any assurance they would have anyone to navigate them through their financial headwaters. This young man was being asked to build trust with a firehose in his arms. After her death, her staff was stretched to the limit. Certainly, her B/D worked significantly harder than it otherwise would to retain her clients. Money was hemorrhaging. Accounts were transferring. There were no winners. The result was not only terrible but *unnecessary* for all concerned.

Liz opted for the default plan—*cessation*—when she could have just as easily opted for a plan that would have been a win for everyone—*succession*. In the end, we all make a choice. Succession, or cessation, the choice is yours.

Chapter 4

There Is Another Way

E ven though Vancouver is about 3,000 miles (5,000 kilometers) from South Florida, Ken and I became good long-distance friends through our mutual association with the Million Dollar Round Table (MDRT). Ken was very thoughtful. He was the consummate phlegmatic—cool, calm, and collected—but passionate at the same time. He just did everything in an untroubled way.

After Ken had been in the business awhile, he met another financial advisor who had recently moved back to Vancouver after a stint working in Toronto. Jim left Ontario to return to his native British Columbia to start an independent insurance and investment advisory practice. Ken was thrilled to work on his own, but Jim was very persuasive and encouraged Ken to help him start the new firm. The idea of working with Jim to develop a team of advisors was appealing to Ken because he envisioned being part of a larger firm, with multiple advisors and staff, rather than a solo practitioner.

When Ken and Jim became business associates, you could hardly call them partners. Initially, they had, for all intents and purposes, two separate businesses under one roof, each with their own clients and staff. However, over time, they saw the unique advantages associated with creating a financial planning firm similar to a large law firm. They formed a corporation and began recruiting other advisors and staff to join the practice. Before long, they had recruited nearly a dozen advisors and had over 30 employees.

Establishing an Enterprise

Rather than solo practitioners sharing space, they envisioned an enterprise, creating significant value for every shareholder in the firm. The one thing they realized early on was by pooling revenues, they drove profits up for both the advisors and the firm. As Jim told me, their goal was to find advisors with a "more than ordinary interest in the affairs of the firm" and grant them shares based on their financial contribution to the company. To ensure the firm was profitable, the company kept a percentage of the top-line revenue and structured a payout schedule of up to 75% of the revenue to the advisor/shareholder. This structure allowed the staff to be employed by the firm and assured the company could provide its employees with excellent employee benefits. It also helped the advisors manage their income in the most tax-advantaged way possible. Rather than be associated with a broker/dealer group, they established their own B/D. Most importantly, the advisors did not have to be concerned with operations, but rather could focus on strictly advising their clients.

The shareholders have been—and remain—consummate professionals both for their clients and themselves. Not only do they advise their clients to create business continuity plans in the event the client becomes critically ill, dies, or otherwise wants to leave and/or sell their interest in their company, they do the same for themselves. They recommend that their clients own significant sums of life and disability insurance. Their business continuation plans are properly insured, as well.

Be on the Lookout for Successors

From their beginning, Ken and Jim were proactively on the lookout for successors. Over time, they came up with a program, which is still in operation, to recruit advisors, including many relatively recent college graduates, to work directly under the tutelage of one or more of the partners for a period of about five years. During this timeframe, partners work directly with the junior associate, delegating work as the junior associate learns the business firsthand from a partner in a type of modern apprenticeship. Within this period, the junior associate is expected to earn an advanced business credential at the firm's expense—e.g., Certified Financial Planner (CFP), Chartered Life Underwriter (CLU), Chartered Financial Consultant (ChFC), or a master's degree in any number of related specialties. The goal is to ensure every advisor is trained with the same methodology and simultaneously becomes certified in the profession. Furthermore, they expect their aspiring advisors to become active in the industry and community. In other words, they only seek individuals who have a passion to become a consummate professional.

Business succession was always front of mind for Ken and Jim. Both men executed personal succession plans; however, they each exited the firm in especially different ways. Nevertheless, their leaving did not weaken the firm. Rather, the enterprise became even stronger under the leadership of their successors.

As said, their respective exits came under quite different circumstances. After being in business for over 30 years, Ken was enjoying unprecedented success. To his credit, he remained the same kind and humble man he was when the two men joined forces decades earlier. Then *it* happened. He went in for a physical examination, and the physician came back with the kind of news no one wants to hear.

You Have Cancer

Unlike Liz, Ken's cancer was treatable. He was given several years before succumbing to the illness. The benefit of time, along with the succession plan he established before he was ill, allowed him to transition his business smoothly—long before he passed. There were two aspects to his plan. First, he committed his estate to sell his interest in the firm back to the company after he died. Second, he entered into an agreement with two of his shareholder partners to buy his book of business with a payout structured over several years. This two-part strategy allowed him to gracefully bow out and focus solely on his health. Because of the seamlessness of the transition, the interruption to his clients was minimal.

The contrast between his exit and the exit of Liz is remarkable. None of his clients left the firm because of his illness and ultimate death. He and his family received the full value of his book as well as the value of his shares in the business. The life insurance the firm owned on his behalf provided liquidity to fund the purchase of his company shares and significantly benefited the business. Although his wife was devasted by the loss of the love of her life, Ken's planning kept her from the financial devastation she might otherwise have experienced when Ken went to be with his Lord.

A Successful Non-Urgent Exit

Coincidentally, while Ken was fighting his cancer, Jim was asked to serve on the MDRT Executive Committee. Serving on the Executive Committee is a five-year commitment that takes you around the world in service of the Million Dollar Round Table. The five members of the MDRT Executive Committee spend nearly half of their life on the road during those five years. Throughout his service to MDRT, Jim realized, if he desired, he could easily transition his clientele to one or more of his associates who were overseeing his clients while he was traveling and exit the business.

Even though Jim was only 62, he was keen to start the next chapter of his life. He had seen how the planning Ken did served him well. Ken's exit was not traumatic—either to his clients, the staff, his successors, or the firm. Unlike Ken, Jim was the firm's CEO. He was responsible for managing his clients' accounts and the general operation of the enterprise as well. While serving on the MDRT Executive Committee, Jim recruited two associates he could trust with the affairs of his clients. When he made the decision to leave the firm, he had two successors in place to purchase his client book and a CEO-in-waiting to assume the leadership role after he stepped down.

When you compare the results of Jim's departure from his firm to the departure of Liz, albeit under vastly different circumstances, the importance of ending with the beginning in mind becomes self-evident. Liz's business never had a chance. Ken and Jim's result was a win for all concerned. The major difference was Ken and Jim's early decision to establish a *firm* in lieu of separate one-man bands. They created a viable enterprise able to sustain itself for generations to come. Liz, on the other hand, established a profitable sole proprietorship. She was an amazing one-woman band, but when she no longer made the music, everything stopped. Indeed, her death swept away all she had ever built.

Contingency Planning Setting up for Succession

Both Ken and Jim had contingency plans in place long before they were ready to exit. A contingency plan is an agreement to protect the firm ahead of either an advisor's death, disability, or retirement from the practice. When a contingency plan is in place, transitioning the practice to new leadership is a far less stressful process.

Another important piece in contingency planning is the introduction of junior associates to clients early in their tenure. Introducing a junior associate to clients well in advance of the founder's exit helps to ensure a warm handoff down the road. The one essential piece that is often overlooked is the advantage of converting a solo operation to an enterprise as early as possible. Liz, who lacked a contingency plan and was a solo operation, had nothing in place to protect against her sudden departure. On the other hand, Ken and Jim were an enterprise with a plan in place to protect them and the firm, and the results of their respective departures were vastly different.

> "When a contingency plan is in place, transitioning the practice to new leadership is a far less stressful process."

It is estimated more than 90% of financial advisors operate as solo practitioners, and the same is true for virtually all small businesses. Even when it appears advisors are part of a common firm, they are often solo practices sharing expenses. For a practice to have a chance of surviving the death, disability, or retirement of the original practitioner, there must be a successor in place who is obvious to clients and with whom clients are comfortable before the founder leaves.

Liz was a highly productive, successful solo producer. Her death created a vacuum that her company was not prepared to overcome. Even with great staff, *she* was the business. This is why, even under the best of circumstances, while not impossible, it can be difficult to successfully sell and transition a solo practice to another individual who is not part of the practice prior to the triggering event leading to the founder's departure.

Finding an Aspirant

Since most clientele of small companies affiliate based on their relationship with the business owner rather than the firm, it takes a special person to step in and keep the clients from moving elsewhere when the business owner departs. Furthermore, it takes a founder committed to allowing a successor to take the lead while staying on for a time as they execute a *warm handoff* to the successor. Therefore, the first step in contingency planning is to find an aspirant.

At a minimum, practitioners should be looking to add younger associates to the practice they can mentor as aspirants. As strange as this may sound on the surface, it is in your best interest to find someone more qualified than yourself! I knew Mags was the right person to succeed me when a client told me, "You know, Don, I really like you, but I *love* Steve." That said, Mags worked with me for almost 15 years before he succeeded me.

If you are not willing to be a mentor, merging with another practice or having another person merge with you is a great way to help secure a transition. The goal of all this planning is to make it easy for clients to stay! As I said earlier, as tempting as it may be, do not wait too long. While you do not want to be hasty, it is always better to be too early than too late. Do your best to find a potential successor with similar values. While you need not be clones or have the same personality or temperament, having the same fundamental values is essential. While Steve and I have vastly different personalities, our values are exceptionally congruent. As important as values may be, if the mentor does not have total belief in the protégé, neither will anyone else.

Start looking early and often. The earlier you have people in place and the more people you have to choose from allows for mistakes. My original aspirant, Steve Scalici, was not the right person. Discovering that early on was a huge advantage. As a result, even though his departure was a huge blow to the business and me personally, it gave us the luxury of being able to say, "No harm, no foul. Let's start looking for the person who is right for us."

Listening

When you are establishing your contingency plans, it is imperative to listen to the people around you. Do not overrule the people who believe in you and whom you trust. Over the years, I have listened when my assistant, Kathy, or my wife, Grace, pulled me aside to let me know when I was playing the fool. Years before our merger, I arranged for Mags to take on the responsibility of minding many of our existing clients. I was looking for the clients and staff to give their thumbs-up to my choice of a successor—*and they did*.

In my experience, the best transitions happen when clients are excited for you. *Listen to your clients!* For the most part, clients love the idea the proprietor is preparing to start another chapter while at the same time looking out for their best interests by attempting to find a like-minded successor. The worst thing a founder can do is leave clients *hoping* the company has a transition plan that is not going to impact them negatively. Always position the contingent transition plan positively. The clients should see this as the start of something even better. One day, once you are retired and doing other things outside the framework of the business, you want to see a client or colleague and have them say, "Thank you! It has been amazing working with your successor!" You *never* want to hear someone say, "Oh, he or she is OK," because *just OK is not* OK! Listen to the people that have your back. They will tell you whether the candidate you have in mind is the right candidate… *if you listen*.

Say It Out Loud

My father used to tell my siblings and me, "Say it out loud!" Dad believed most people rarely say what is *really* going on in their minds. Verbalizing plans makes them more tangible. When you say things out loud, it becomes

self-evident whether the plan is
solid or ridiculous. Saying what
you intend to do and then memo-
rializing those intentions in writing is the next step in creating a

"Say it out loud!"

worthwhile contingency plan that will work when the time comes to execute
the agreement.

Just because someone thinks about something does not mean anyone
else knows what they are thinking. This clearly plays out in contingency
discussions involving the "what happens if" or the "what happens when"
type of conversation. The problem is that even though these conversations
are important, they are rarely urgent. It is easy to push contingency planning
to the back burner to be forgotten or ignored. The trouble with the back
burner is it has just enough heat under it to set the pan on fire and create
an unintended emergency.

It is imperative to speak freely with colleagues, staff, clients, and,
most of all, any potential successor. In our case, we ended up needing two
successors—one to work with the clients and another to run the business.
However, we only discovered this through frank conversations with our
key people, including Mags. What we learned was Mags had no interest
in running the business; he just wanted to advise clients. As a result, I
started looking for a second person willing to partner with Mags and
ultimately found Chad. Chad, on the other hand, loves the business of
the business. When I met Chad, one of our first discussions concerned the
ground rules of any merger we might consider. In the merger, it was our
intent to create a scenario where the clients would be managed by Mags
and Chad would oversee the operations of the business and the RIA. It
was a good fit from the start, predicated on everyone saying what they
were thinking, out loud!

Get It in Writing!

It has been said that an unwritten goal is merely a wish. It is, therefore, not only paramount to say things out loud, but to put agreements in writing. After discussing a subject, memorialize what is said in writing. However, as with the discussion stage, make sure the writing stage is as collaborative as the discussion. The principal and the potential successor should pen a separately constructed first draft of what each one thinks was said. Do not marvel if the drafts are considerably different. Everyone writes from their own perspective. This creates an excellent place to start and hammer out the details. Remember: The goal at this stage is to create a contingency agreement to protect the company and the founder from either death, disability, or the desire to exit. This is not the final agreement to sell the company. That will come down the road.

While each of the items put on paper will get the process off to a good start, make sure to work on this collaboratively. Do not fear getting selected clients, staff, and people who know the founder and successor well involved in the process. Once a deal is agreed upon in principle, communicate with your key clients and staff precisely how the transition will benefit *them*. It is understood the deal is going to benefit the founder and the successor. Clients and staff want to know how this is going to impact them.

Action Steps

There are numerous action items to complete before a succession plan can be established and ultimately put in motion.

1. Identify a Successor

As I said above, the first step in creating a workable plan is to identify an aspirant you think is a qualified successor. The best candidate should be working with you when you establish the plan. However, it has been my experience that competitors can have a contingency plan set up between themselves that allows one company to buy out the other in the event one principal dies, becomes disabled, or wants to retire.

Over the years, I have hired numerous advisors. I told you about Steve Scalici earlier. Sometimes you may think a person is your long-term successor when they may be a short-term contingency instead. There was a period shortly before Scalici decided to leave when I suffered a serious respiratory ailment. It left me powerless to speak and ultimately put me out of business for several months. Steve stepped in and covered for me as I recovered, and was a tremendous blessing! Whether the aspirant is there to support the principal during a short-term challenge or as a permanent successor, to be effective, a candidate must be capable and willing to succeed the founder should one of the three triggering events, death, disability, or retirement, occur.

2. Purchase Life and Disability Insurance

While some presume every financial advisor, insurance agent, attorney, CPA, or other financial practitioner has adequate insurance coverage, in my experience, many are woefully underinsured. If not in place already, make sure there is adequate personal life and disability insurance, as well as corporate coverage, on the founder.

Obviously, life insurance can be expensive, especially if it is a permanent policy, but insurance is vital to the success of any plan should the founder die or become disabled prematurely. The life and disability insurance Ken owned made all the difference in the success of his business continuity plan. If I were a successor, I would rue the day I ended up in business with the founder's spouse, children, grandchildren, or worse, all the above! Adequate insurance can make all the difference.

When it comes to a disability, keep in mind most disabilities are not permanent. They often last a short time—a few weeks or months, rather than years. Merely having a person prepared to take over on an interim basis might be enough to augment for a short-term disability. Permanent disability is another matter. There are numerous insurance products available for this contingency. Some pay out a monthly amount for either life or a specific number of years. Other plans can pay a lump sum after the insured satisfies an elimination period—an elected amount of time the insured must be disabled—before the policy pays benefits. Remove this pan from the back burner and investigate insurance options. Depending on where a business owner is in the life of the business, this could be a critical piece in executing the plan.

3. Generate Recurring Revenue

We are going to discuss this at length in the next chapter, but it essential to have a firm that is attractive to a buyer. One of the best ways to make a company attractive is by having a stream of regular, recurring income. Now, hear me correctly; I did not say focus on getting clients to pay a recurring *fee*. Setting up accounts based solely on charging a client recurring fees may or may not be in the client's best interest. Instead, find clients who need the firm's *ongoing help* on a recurring basis, and bill them accordingly. This is not only good for the client; it is a best practice of sustainable businesses.

I have a friend who practices corporate and real property law. She focuses on clients who need her services frequently. She has purposefully chosen clients who will need *ongoing* legal services while avoiding transactional clients—those who need her for one transaction and are never seen again. In practice, this means charging ongoing fees for ongoing services. In a CPA firm, it might mean finding clients who need ongoing help, rather than simply doing a tax return. In an advisory firm, this typically means finding clients who desire active management for a stated or percentage ongoing fee.

4. Bring Succession Planning to the Front Burner

It is never too soon to make succession planning a *front-burner* issue. Frankly, if I were a young person today wanting to be a financial advisor, I would be searching out a successful advisor 20 to 30 years older than me in need of a successor. If I were a solo practitioner, I would be conversely searching for several potential successors and creating an enterprise rather than remaining a one-man band.

> *"It is never too soon to make succession planning a front-burner issue."*

A succession plan is not worth the paper it is written on, however, if all the players—including the named successor, clients, staff, and even your vendors—are not a part of the process. Notwithstanding, thinking a firm does not need to be concerned about business continuity is a big mistake … because everything in life will ultimately end.

Including this chapter!

CHAPTER 5

SUCCESSION MATTERS

J im is a financial advisor who started and spent the first two decades of his career with a major wirehouse. Soon after the 2008-2009 financial crisis, he made the decision to join an independent broker/dealer group. Within days of his resignation, the wirehouse branch manager put on what Jim now calls "the full-court press" to keep his clients from moving their accounts.

Jim was one of the largest producers in the office. Even though he had been with the wirehouse for over a decade, he had no idea how zealous the manager would become when it came to keeping Jim from moving any of his accounts from the wirehouse. Because the manager saw every client as a client of the house, he reminded Jim, he was prohibited from taking client records when he resigned. Indeed, the removal of any client information, including the books and records of the client activity, would be a violation of his contract, and such a violation would be reported on his U-5 Termination Notice provided to FINRA when a registered person terminates from a broker/dealer.[1]

The manager assigned a team of 10 advisors to contact, visit, and, in any way possible, convince the clients to forsake Jim and remain with the wirehouse. It was 10 on one, and it was *not* pretty. Jim, however, had something much more valuable than books and records—he had *relational capital*. His clients trusted him, and many had dealt with him for a decade or more. He was a large producer, not because of the wirehouse, but because people trusted him.

Trust Matters

Trust is why people followed Jim's recommendations. Trust was his secret weapon because trust creates relational capital. Jim had it—the manager and his minions did not. Jim read his contract from cover to cover for the first time a week before he resigned. He did not like what he read. Nevertheless, he was intent on living up to it. His clients ("his people," as Jim affectionately called them), he determined, would move with him because they trusted him. His Blackberry held the personal phone number and email address of every person he advised. Jim went through his phone and began spending the relational capital he had accrued for just this moment. As Jim put it, "His people listened to him."

I met Jim about 10 years after this event. He shared the story repeated above, and when I asked him about his succession plan, he chuckled. He said he had a plan once, but it had soured. The plan was to add several advisors and grow the company into a sustainable business he could sell when he was ready to retire. He recruited several advisors, but not one of them stayed. They either left the business or decided to strike out on their own. He also struggled to find good administrative help and a reliable sales assistant. In fact, he had hired and replaced a half-dozen administrative people. He has become a classic one-man band. Jim does not believe succession matters. He looks through a lens intent on seeing only the obstacles to succession:

- Capable millennials, in his estimation, are in short supply.
- No one is loyal anymore. They are always looking for *greener pastures*.
- The last thing he wants is another project. As he aged, his energy has waned. He is worn out.

"Why bother?" Jim told me. "My succession plan is easy—either I die, or my clients do."

Succession Planning Matters

When it comes to succession, the first question a business owner needs to answer is *why*. Does it really matter? Jim is convinced it does not matter. Jim is content to simply earn a good living and ride it out for as long as it lasts.

Without realizing it, Jim has already entered a plan for his succession. It was not a transaction with a qualified younger person capable of growing what he started; it was a transaction with himself. He executed a succession plan where he was both the buyer and the seller. The transaction was effectuated for the sum of whatever he earns over the remaining part of his career … and nothing else. Frankly, Jim's cessation plan is the succession plan of the masses.

> *"When it comes to succession, the first question a business owner needs to answer is why."*

Financial advisors are walking enigmas. We share our client's greatest milestones and their deepest tragedies. For years, we help people map out their hopes for the future. We advise them on how to transition from being dependent on making money to allowing assets to make money on their behalf. We advise people on how to leverage those assets to gain greater choices and transition smoothly into the next stage of life.

If only every advisor advised themselves in the same way they advised their clients.

Advisors, as a group, tend to be utilitarian. They have a propensity to be comfortable with matters of the hands (*how* to do things) and matters of the head (*what* to do). For many, the comfort level diminishes when it comes to matters of the heart (*why* we do what we do). Succession is a matter of the heart. No one is going to let their baby go unless they know why. Moreover, changing matters of the heart is difficult because it is an individual decision everyone needs to make for themselves.

Succession matters. Just working until you cannot work any longer is a waste of relational capital! Building a sustainable business, which I define as a salable business, and then selling it is a volitional choice—a matter of will—and it can only happen when the *why* question has been settled. Building a sustainable, salable, multi-generational firm is doable, but it takes work and a commitment to see it through. Nonetheless, there are things a proprietor can do to make the operation attractive to buyers. Implementing these ideas will not guarantee a business will either continue or be sold to a buyer in the future. Everything in business is without guarantees. As every entrepreneur knows, there is always something unforeseen on the horizon (like a global pandemic, for starters) conspiring to change everything. Know this: When you have determined **why** making your most important asset marketable is important, implementing those strategies will make sense.

Sustainability Matters

A business cannot be considered sustainable unless two things are true.

First, the business must be attractive enough to a successor that they are willing to pay the owner for it. Second, the founder must be committed to being something more than a one-man band. We will discuss the first matter now and the second in the following chapter.

I love growing orchids. Misconceptions about orchid fragility and sustainability abound. Like most perennials, with proper care, orchids can last for many years. Orchids do not bloom continuously. Their natural lifecycle differs from plant to plant. However, one thing is constant: They are either growing, or they are dying. While I am not saying I can make a direct correlation to businesses, the one thing that is true about both is when an orchid is in full bloom, everyone wants to buy it. Conversely, when it is nothing more than a stick in a pot, no one gives it a second look. The most they might do is ask, "Why are you keeping that thing?"

My mom loved orchids ... *when they were in bloom*. However, she wanted nothing to do with orchids when they went dormant. She would consistently call and ask me for a new plant because she was sure the old one was dead. I cannot tell you how many times I would bring her a plant, and she would say, "Oh, this is beautiful. The flowers are so bright. It reminds me of the orchid that died last year." Of course, the reason it reminded her of the orchid that "died" last year was it actually was the orchid that "died" last year. After a while, I gave up trying to explain. I just let her enjoy the plant when it was in bloom. Then I would take it back when it was "dead" and replace it with another plant that had previously "died" and remarkably resurrected from the dead. I still smile when I think of all the orchids she was convinced were dead but were far from it.

This is also true for a business. Buyers are not going to pay top dollar for either an orchid or a business that is not in full bloom. Unlike orchids, which must go dormant to rebloom the following season, with proper maintenance and care, a sustainable business can remain perpetually in bloom. I have talked to many businesspeople during the pandemic. I assumed most would be struggling mightily because of the shutdowns. While many were doing poorly, an equal number had adapted to the crisis and were recording historic sales and profits. How is that possible? Did no one tell them we were in a pandemic?

Common Characteristics of Sustainable Businesses

Dr. Frank is my chiropractor. In the over 20 years I have known him, I have watched him grow into a tremendous entrepreneur. However, I was never more impressed with him and his leadership than during the COVID-19 pandemic. Starting in March 2020, the governor of Florida began issuing executive orders regarding the COVID crisis. Eventually, he ordered all non-essential businesses to close indefinitely to "stop the spread" of the virus. It was initially unclear if chiropractors were essential businesses and many chiropractors, along with dentists, therapists, and other non-critical care providers shuttered their offices.

Frank made an executive decision to remain open, albeit while implementing the guidelines issued by the CDC, until he was directly ordered to close. At the beginning of April, the U.S. Department of Homeland Security declared chiropractors were essential. Every chiropractor could reopen. For a variety of reasons, many did not. In the meantime, Frank's office remained open and his phone began ringing off the hook. Patients calling their chiropractors found the offices closed indefinitely. Many started looking around and found Frank and his team were available. Every patient from another doctor was told, "When your doctor's facility reopens, we encourage you to go back." In due time, the other chiropractors started reopening, but many of the patients never went back. They enjoyed the experience with Frank and his team and became permanent patients. 2020 was a horrible year for a lot of his competitors. For Frank, it was his best year ever.

Make Your Own Luck

Frank has a formidable characteristic of sustainable businesses—*they make their own luck*. Making your own luck begins with being a contrarian. These contrarians put themselves in the right situations and take advantage of the right opportunities. Ultimately, these "lucky ones" accomplish what others only wish they could achieve by taking chances others did not take and then outworking their competition.

The individuals, companies, and industries that make their own luck do it by helping out instead of looking for a handout. They become stepping stones for others instead of stepping all over others. They are curious enough to look for different ways to overcome challenges and do not fear the randomness of a possible solution.

> *"The individuals, companies, and industries that make their own luck do it by helping out instead of looking for a handout."*

I have found those who make their own luck are people and organizations who:

- Are willing to take a chance when other people are not.
- Remain positive while others bitterly complain.
- Outwork others.
- Stay in the present.
- Accept failure.

There are always going to be things out of your control. Had Frank received a cease and desist order, he would have needed to close. He did not, and so people thought he was lucky. Was he? Maybe, but like every sustainable business, he took a chance, remained positive, worked hard, stayed in the present, and although he knew it might fail, he was not afraid of failing. He made his own luck.

Transparency

Sustainable businesses, those people look to buy, operate with complete transparency. They eliminate the mushroom syndrome—keeping everyone in the dark and feeding them with manure. Transparency, what I call *operating in the light*, makes it easy for buyers to be attracted to a company.

> *"Entrepreneurs should never ask, 'Where did the money go?'"*

Operating in the light begins with keeping impeccably accurate books and records. Accurate books reveal where revenues are derived and where money is spent. Entrepreneurs should never ask, "Where did the money go?" They should know! They should be able to hit a button and pull up an accurate accounting of the actual numbers of the company instantaneously. Every report, e.g., transactional and recurring revenue, net profit after expenses for the month, quarter, year to date, last year, and period versus prior years, and its current balance sheet should be available at any time. Many businesspeople are reticent or ashamed to reveal to anyone their books and records. A business is not sustainable if it is not fully transparent financially. A transparent company could go through an audit tomorrow, and the numbers would not change because they are operating in the light.

Further, do not keep financial secrets. Secrets are the bane of sustainability because they are rooted in lies. That is why financial secrets are unhealthy. They force not only the owner, but the financial employees to operate in the dark instead of the light. In the same way a plant needs light to grow, a business cannot grow without absolute transparency. It is an old saying, but honesty is the best policy.

Look, the purpose of this section is not to tell anyone how to live. It is merely to point out that transparency is not a hindrance to success; it is an impetus for it. There are always going to be negative consequences for operating in the dark or on the edge of darkness. One of the consequences of operating secretively is no one will want to buy your business for anywhere near what it could be worth! Dr. Guy Baker, a past president of the Million Dollar Round Table and author of a half-dozen books on investing and practice management, once told me, "There is no new money." What he meant was the money the buyer pays for a business comes exclusively from the money the buyer makes from the assets of the company. If a successor does not have accurate numbers, how can they know what to pay for the business? The value does not come from the sky. It comes from efficient, scalable processes made repeatable and profitable by operating transparently. Too many businesses have a myriad of unnecessary expenses created by the founders to suit their myopic way of life. Operating transparently is not sexy, but it is highly attractive to buyers.

A Differentiating Value Proposition

It is imperative that firms pay attention to what differentiates them from their competitors. Indeed, a company's value proposition is its taproot. A firm's value proposition tells clients what makes this firm special and the best choice for them. Every firm offers essentially the same products and services. So, what sets one firm apart from the competition? Every firm needs to determine its unique value proposition and nurture it with great care.

I recently heard about a group of entrepreneurs who had one of the best value propositions I have ever seen. As a result, they are securing clients all over the United States and have set the firm apart in their unique niche. The group works exclusively on behalf of dentists. They are completely invested in understanding the needs of this one group. If a doctor decides to use their firm, they become the doctor's agent for all things financial. Unlike their competitors, who handle one aspect of the work, this group has brought together talent from the four corners of the financial services industry and beyond. If the doctor needs help with equipment, real estate, investments, insurance, loan acquisition, or any other question, the doctor calls the company for assistance. Their technology solutions are state of the art. They have gone out of their way to hire some of the finest and brightest personnel available. They are as different as they are focused. They know the needs of this group of doctors right down to what brand furniture and equipment is the finest deal for their patient rooms and the best way to manage their employee benefits and retirement plans.

> *"Sustainable businesses have a value proposition that is not only powerfully attractive to potential customers, it is equally attractive to prospective buyers and successors."*

Sustainable businesses set themselves apart and are uniquely different from the competition in a positive way. There is coming a day when someone will be begging them to sell what they have created and built. Sustainable businesses have a value proposition that is not only powerfully attractive to potential customers, it is equally attractive to prospective buyers and successors.

Positive Work Environment

Zig Ziglar rightly said, "Your attitude, *not your aptitude*, will determine your altitude." A positive attitude is at the root of sustainability. It is part of the company DNA. Nothing kills sustainability faster and more completely than negativity and a root of bitterness. Do not underestimate both the value of a positive work environment and the destructive influence of a negative work environment. A positive work environment is an absolute success predictor. It trumps virtually all statistical measurements. In his book, *Learned Optimism*, Martin Seligman writes that negative people get sick more often, are divorced more frequently, and raise kids who get in more trouble. Dr. Seligman also found people who are negative tend to be poorer than those who have positive attitudes. In a study of 1,500 people, Seligman wrote, over 80% took jobs for the money, and less than 20% said money was secondary—they simply loved what they chose to do. Two decades later, the 1,500 people produced 101 millionaires. Amazingly, only one of those millionaires came from the 80% who chose a job because of the financial rewards, and 100 came from the group that said money was secondary, and they chose their work because they loved what they chose to do.[2]

In the same book, Seligman writes only about a third of millionaires graduated from college or university. He also wrote about 70% of CEOs graduated in the bottom half of their class. Seligman confirmed what Zig Ziglar preached. Attitude, *more than their aptitude*, determines altitude.

I used to work with a lady who was fond of saying, "I am just telling it the way it is," after she ripped you up one side and down the other. She also liked to say, "I cannot change. That is just the way God made me." I recommended she read the biography of Abraham Lincoln. Lincoln lost election after election, had a horrible marriage, a nation fighting against itself under his watch, and the issue of slavery beguiling his presidency, yet he chose a positive attitude over bitterness. In fact, if anyone had a reason to be bitter, it was President Lincoln. Bitterness was not how he dealt with his adversity. He chose to encourage those around him and build people up rather than tear them down. Most of all, he showed respect for other people. His respect for disregarded people explains why he is considered by many the greatest president in American history.

At the head of every sustainable business is leadership that cares, respects, and positively impacts those around them. Mostly, they love to win, but are not afraid to lose. I recently watched a series on Michael Jordan and his stint with the Chicago Bulls. Prior to Michael joining the Bulls, the team had never won a championship—Zero! Before he left, they had won six! Since he left, zero again. Michael has a winner's attitude—*he loves to win*. While he hates to lose, he is not afraid of it. However, he has a greater love for winning than a hate for losing. Because he loved to win, occasionally, he would rub people—usually, those not committed to winning—the wrong way. Nevertheless, at his core, he refused to be bitter. He just wanted to win.

New Growth

Sustainable businesses are always adding new clients and new personnel—they are always growing. Too many mature businesses quench growth, plateau, and then regress. If an organization is not experiencing growth organically, it is dying. Dying businesses, like dying plants, are unsustainable. A plant that appears to be dying can be saved if it is given the proper care before it is unsalvageable. Are you going to pay top dollar for either a dying plant or a dying business? Probably not. If you stop regression early enough, a dying business can be rebuilt. Notwithstanding, do not quench growth.

> *"If an organization is not experiencing growth organically, it is dying."*

If you are concerned about growth, consider this five-point checklist:

First, be proactive. Mature businesses often struggle with resting on their laurels and must fight growing comfortable with success and neglecting growth. If you are not adding new clients, it is either because your value proposition is weak or you are not asking, or both.

Second, avoid the activity trap. Be careful not to fall into this trap Stephen Covey wrote about. Activity does not always equate to results. In the absence of clearly defined, quantifiable processes, everyone from the CEO to the clerks will find themselves focused on activity and run the risk of being enslaved to activity.

Third, prospect existing clients. The best place to prospect for new business is with existing clients. Russell Conwell was a prolific 19th and early 20th century lecturer, lawyer, pastor, and founder of Temple University in Philadelphia. His most highly regarded lecture was entitled *Acres of Diamonds*. It is said he gave the lecture over 5,000 times! The short version of this great story is this:

Al Hafed had a nice farm in modern-day Iraq and was content with his wealth. One day a priest related how the world was made, including the formation of all the rocks, the earth, the precious metals and stones. He told the farmer with just a few diamonds he could have, not one, but many farms. Al Hafed suddenly became discontented with what he had acquired in his life.

He sold all his land and went across the Middle East and Europe in search of diamonds. After searching the world in vain, he had nothing but the rags on his body. When a large wave came in from the sea, he was happily swept under by it.

Meanwhile, the man who had bought the farmer's land noticed a glint in the stream on his property. It was a diamond. Not one, but one of the largest finds of diamonds ever—the mines of Golconda which had not one or two, but acres of diamonds.[3]

While not 5,000, I have had the privilege of sharing this story numerous times since I first heard it over 40 years ago. The moral of the story is before you go around the world prospecting for diamonds, make sure you have mined all the diamonds already in your own backyard.

Fourth, count the cost. A few years ago, I decided to build a house. Before we moved a mound of earth, we met with the architect, drafted the plans, and calculated what it was going to cost to make sure we could finish. Can you imagine building a home and saying, "Hey guys, let's start digging, and we will work out the details as we go along!" Still, I meet people every day who never count the cost when it comes to growing their business.

Counting the cost always goes beyond the cost in dollars and cents. Beyond the financial cost, there is the cost of time. Is this going to cost relational capital, or some other intangible cost? While there may be a myriad of costs necessary to meet every objective, do not fall prey to paralysis by analysis. Examine the costs and make sure you are willing to spend what it takes to finish.

Finally, keep playing the game. Every team turns the ball over occasionally. When LeBron James played basketball for the Miami Heat, I personally witnessed one of the greatest recoveries from a turnover I have ever seen. LeBron was dribbling the ball when the opposing player reached in and swatted the ball from his hand and made a beeline to the other end. Instead of demeaning himself for his bad play, LeBron chased the guy down, leaped as the other player was airborne, and made a perfect block of the shot. Even writing this, I am experiencing the same surge of adrenaline I felt when I witnessed that block.

"Making mistakes is just part of the game—and one of the reasons we play at all."

Making mistakes is just part of the game—and one of the reasons we play at all.

This little checklist has consistently course-corrected our firm and me personally for years. Take the time to memorize them, and if you are struggling to get back on track in building the business:

1. Be more proactive and less reactive.
2. Be less concerned with activity and more concerned with a process that brings results.
3. Remember *Acres of Diamonds*.
4. Count the cost, and above all …
5. Keep playing the game!

Good Husbandry

Avoid the path of my friend, Jim, who believes succession does not matter. Succession matters! Trust, planning and sustainability matter! There is no magic to building a business other people will form a line to buy one day. It just requires being willing to do what others are too afraid to try—being transparent, having a value proposition that differentiates you from the crowd, and creating a place people want to come and be a part of every day.

Build a business that cares for other people the way a nurseryman cultivates his plantings. It is what the agriculturalists call *good husbandry*, which is not only the cultivation or production of plants or animals, but the control or judicious use of resources.[4] Indeed, the word *husband* means to "use (resources) economically." Be a husband of your business, and people will be lining up to take your place once you are ready to go. Intuitively, businesspeople understand the importance of husbandry in a business. While being responsible for cultivating clientele, controlling and using resources judiciously, good husbandry looks to cultivate a new generation of leadership by either mentoring or diligently seeking the right person(s) to continue to *husband* the business in the future.

CHAPTER 6

FINDING THE RIGHT SUCCESSOR

The sixth book of the Bible is entitled *Joshua*. It chronicles Israel's conquest of Canaan and the leadership of Moses' aspirant, Joshua. Before Moses died, he handpicked Joshua to be his successor and lead Israel into the promised land. Joshua was Moses' understudy for 40 years. Joshua and Caleb were the only adults who left Egypt and stepped foot into Canaan. Joshua was a man of great faith, confidence, and uncompromising leadership. In the first nine sentences of his narrative, he writes he was told by God to be strong, courageous, and fearless, not once, but three separate times. Joshua was keenly aware of the need to stand firm in his beliefs.[1] Later in the book, when the people are ready to desert both him and the God of Israel, Joshua boldly stands up to his adversaries and says, "I gave you a land on which you had not labored and cities that you had not built, and you dwell in them. You eat the fruit of vineyards and [groves of] olives you did not plant." He went on to say, "Choose this day whom you will serve, whether the gods [of] your fathers or of the [people of Canaan], **but, as for me and my house, we will serve the Lord.**"[2]

Joshua, like every great leader, understood the paralytic power of fear. He understood to conquer the *promised land*, he had to be fearless, strong, and courageous—the exact traits every founder should be looking for in their chosen successor.

Find Your Joshua

"Sustainable businesses are started by a Moses and sustained by a Joshua."

Most great businesses are founded by a Moses. Moses took the Israelites out of Egypt, carried down the commandments, and *established* a people. He was not the person called to *sustain* the nation. That was the role of Joshua. Moses knew it, and when it was time, he stepped away and gave the reins to his understudy. Sustainable businesses are started by a Moses and sustained by a Joshua.

If you are a Moses, what are you doing to find your Joshua? Moses found Joshua when he was young and trained him for nearly 40 years to be his successor. While I do not think you need to mentor someone for 40 years, the earlier you are looking for a successor, the better. Moses realized he was not immortal. He picked Joshua early and developed him well.

Products can never differentiate companies because every firm has essentially the same arrows in its quiver. The ability to motivate people to act is what differentiates firms and leaders alike.

The question remains, where do I find a Joshua? Surprisingly, he or she (or they) is usually right under your nose. They may be the person you met at a community meeting or at a conference you attended. They may be a member of a mutual organization. They could be the person sitting next to you at an event you are attending, or an intern from the local university.

In other words, if you want to find your Joshua, just pay attention. Every Joshua is found uniquely. Keep your eyes and your mind wide open, and your Joshua (potentially several of them) will be revealed in often incomprehensible ways.

S – W – E – A – T

A while back, I developed the leadership acrostic S – W – E – A – T to express the five traits you should be looking for in a leader, *especially* a succession candidate. Leaders whom others are prepared to follow will exemplify these five traits. Find someone who embodies these five qualities:

- Setting their *Sights*
- With a great *Work Ethic*
- Who *Encourages* others
- *Accepts* the things they cannot change, and
- Is *Tenacious*,

and you might have just found your Joshua.

Sights

The first trait common to both the Joshua of old and of today is that they set their sights on the finish line. Even when something goes wrong, they are focused on the goal, not the obstacle. When Moses sent 12 men out to scout the land of Canaan, 10 came back concerned about the obstacles. The 10 reported back they could not defeat the people living in the land. The people were stronger. They were bigger. They told Moses they saw giants who made them look like grasshoppers. They were plainly more powerful than the Israelites. On the other hand, Joshua and his cohort, Caleb, told Moses to go at once.

"We can certainly conquer them!" Not once did either Caleb or Joshua express the concerns of their associates, who said there were giants in the land.[3]

Great leaders see the end from the beginning, not the obstacles along the way. They have a clear vision, meaning they focus on opportunities and possibilities, not on what can go wrong. People with clear vision know what they want to do, and by taking inventory of their strengths and weaknesses, they can focus on what they need to do to reach the end goal.

In 1519, Spanish Captain Hernán Cortés landed in Veracruz to begin his conquest of the Americas. After the ships were set at anchor, he ordered his men to burn each one. It has been said that one of his crew laughed, and Cortés ran his sword into the indignant man's throat. Think of the scene as a bloodier version of *Pirates of the Caribbean* with Cortés played by Johnny Depp.

"Retreat is easy when retreat is an option."

Cortés was not returning to Spain. When he lit the ships aflame, he established an irrevocable course. Agree or disagree with his tactic, he demonstrated indisputable leadership and resolute commitment. On the face of it, you might ask, "Wouldn't it make more sense to keep at least one ship around, just in case?" Cortés decided that leaving, quitting, was not an option. He set his sights and set the standard. There are times when a leader needs to publish the order to burn the ships. The lesson of Cortés is clear. Retreat is easy when retreat is an option.

Setting your sights is seeing the end in the beginning and committing to achieve it. While it does not guarantee results, it *does* establish the process. There is nothing more important in life, business, sport—you name it—than having a clear picture of what you *see* being accomplished. Jack Nicklaus said it best. "I never hit a shot," Nicklaus said, "even in practice, without having a very sharp, in-focus picture of it in my head. It is like a color movie. First, I *see* the ball where I want it to finish, nice and high, sitting up on the bright green grass. Then the scene quickly changes. I *see* the ball going there: its path, trajectory, and shape, even its behavior on landing."[4] There is a major difference between GOATs[5] and everyone else. GOATs visualize in ways others do not.

Do not waste time wandering around your own personal Wonderland, hoping someone will suddenly fall into your lap from Somewhere. Proactively look for the right successor, even if succession is down the road. Do not worry about making a mistake. Nicklaus may have seen the shot in his brain, but he still hit lots of errant shots and had to play from unexpected positions from time to time. Do not fear making course corrections along the way, and do not confuse efficiency with effectiveness. Smooth sailing does not mean you are headed in the proper direction. No matter how clear the northbound highway may be, if your goal is to reach Miami (the southernmost exit on I-95), going northbound takes you further from the goal.

Finally, keep in mind the goal is to find a Joshua, not replicate Moses. Find the *right* person who has set their sights on taking the company into the promised land—*find a Joshua!*

> *"Finally, keep in mind the goal is to find a Joshua, not replicate Moses."*

Work Ethic

Jack Nicklaus was 56 years old when Tiger Woods, at age 20, made his professional golf debut. At 56 years old, Jack was obviously no longer playing like he was in his heyday. Then, along came Tiger Woods. Despite Tiger's personal and physical struggles in the middle of his career, along with Nicklaus, he is unquestionably one of the best golfers of all time.

Before his 21st birthday, he won an unprecedented three straight USGA Junior titles and three consecutive USGA Amateur championships—*no one's ever done that!*

After only three years as a professional, Woods became the third leading money winner—of all time—*no one's ever done that!*

He is the only player to ever win four major championship titles consecutively—now known as The Tiger Slam—*no one's ever done that!*

I could go on, but you catch my drift.

Early in his life, Tiger set his sights on becoming the next Nicklaus, and he appears to have pulled it off. No one has won more golf tournaments on the PGA Tour than Tiger Woods—*no one!*

Tiger has an unparalleled work ethic. It is not only what he does on the course, but what he has done *off* the course in preparation of his work on it that is impressive. Woods would routinely spend up to 20 hours or more a week working on his fitness and strength in the gym. He hit thousands of putts, chips, and other shots, honing his game. When his eyesight was suspect, he opted for laser eye surgery. Tiger believed finding his edge off the course gave him the finest opportunity on it.

Golfing professionally is not dissimilar to many vocations. When a professional golfer is playing in a tournament, they spend 4-5 hours a day, four days a week, competing. They spend an even greater amount of time preparing for those 16-20 hours of actual competition. Woods' off-course work ethic revolutionized professional golf. Before Tiger, only a handful of golfers considered a preparation routine remotely similar to Woods. Thanks to Tiger, exercise, diet, swing coaches, and instructors are the new normal in pro golf. Being the best on the course requires being even better when no one is watching. What Tiger showed is his work ethic honed his talent, forced him to be better prepared, and made him seek greater knowledge—three priceless traits of all great leaders.

Talent is priceless. There is little doubt Tiger Woods has talent. I could work twice as hard and never be half as good a golfer as Tiger Woods. Talent is a gift. It is extremely important not to waste it. Tiger's work ethic honed his natural talent, and the combination of talent and work ethic made him indomitable. Help the candidate hone their gift and maximize their talent.

Preparation is priceless. Too many people are not *students of the business.* Find an aspirant who is dedicated to learning the art of the business. On the bright side, anyone can be encouraged to work hard. Everybody is capable of learning how to prepare, study, read, listen to tapes, join webinars, and attend conferences.

Knowledge is also priceless. There is a story told about a student coming to the Greek philosopher, Socrates, seeking knowledge. "What are you willing to do to gain knowledge, my son?" Socrates inquired. The young man, full of gusto, announced to his mentor, "I would sacrifice anything for the knowledge of Socrates."

"Anything?" Socrates asked.

"Most certainly," the student replied, "I would sacrifice anything for the wisdom of Socrates."

The two men were sitting beside a fountain in front of the philosopher's home. Suddenly, Socrates grabbed the young student by the neck and plunged his head beneath the water. The student found himself gasping without any hope of his next breath. Socrates pulled him up and said, "Now—what do you want?"

"Air, Socrates, air! Let me only have air, that I may live."

"Yes, my son," Socrates replied, "You shall have air, and when you desire knowledge the way you desire air, only then will you gain it."[6]

"Do they have the work ethic, coupled with talent, preparation, and knowledge, to become a Joshua?"

The important question when finding a Joshua is:

Do they have the work ethic, coupled with talent, preparation, and knowledge, to become a Joshua?

Encouragement

As you near the end of a long race, your legs ache, your throat is parched, and your body cries out to stop. This is when raving fans are the most valuable. Their encouragement helps you push through the pain to the finish line. Indeed, a word of encouragement offered at the right moment may be the deciding difference between finishing well and collapsing along the way. Everyone needs raving fans! We are better when surrounded by encouragers.

Without encouragement, people tend to lose focus at the slightest adversity. While a certain amount of success can be attained without encouragement, eventually, energy fades. Without encouragement, adversity brings complaint, often leading to a *culture of complaint*. Those brought up in a culture of complaint associate with people who squander their entire lives venting about how bad everything is. They are naturally condescending and are critical of, well, everything! Often, the difference between those who finish the race and those who quit can be directly correlated to whether they exist in a state of encouragement or a culture of complaint.

Encouragement creates positive reciprocity. The person you are encouraging today may well be encouraging you tomorrow. The CEO of my first independent broker/dealer, John Dixon, once told me, "Never burn a bridge in life because you never know when you may have to cross the same bridge again." The value of encouragement cannot be understated.

Encouragement demonstrates you care. It is one of the most powerful ways to lift people up when they feel most alone. Many years ago, my mom started calling me her "heartless son." Whether it is justified or not is still up for debate. I am not a very touchy-feely kind of guy. If I am honest, there are times when I can be pragmatic, if not downright choleric. I am just a grumpy guy looking for a place to grump. My mom thought this was heartless, when, in fact, my expression of care is simply different from, say, my mom's way of expressing care.

The seat of our emotions, *the heart*, consists of three separate and distant parts—intellect, will, and feelings. An intellectual act is rational. An act of the will is volitional. Feelings are emotional. Did you notice intellect and will are singular nouns, but feelings can only be expressed as plural? When it comes to matters of the heart, people respond either rationally (intellect), volitionally (will), or emotionally (feelings).

The rational response appears phlegmatic—calm, unemotional, and cerebral—because it is centered around intellect, what you think. It is not heartless—it is unemotional. The volitional response is a willful or chosen response. Scott Peck, in his book *The Road Less Traveled,* wrote, "Genuine love is volitional rather than emotional. The person who truly loves does so because of a decision to love. This person has made a commitment to be loving whether the loving feeling is present [or not]. Conversely, it is not only possible but necessary for a loving person to avoid acting on *feelings* of love."[7] What Peck was saying is genuine concern for other people, love, does not have to be expressed emotionally. Genuine love is a choice, an act of the will. You do not have to have "that loving feeling" the Righteous Brothers lost when they penned their hit song, to encourage other people. If you do not remember the song, watch *Top Gun* again.

Whether you express love rationally, volitionally, or emotionally, you can still be a great encourager of other people. Encouragers draw other people to themselves and are a great help to those around them. Encouragement is much more than being a cheerleader. Often the greatest encouragement a person can give is just being there, without saying a word.

> *"Often the greatest encouragement a person can give is just being there, without saying a word."*

Even though there is rarely a situation where there is not someone in need of encouragement, a common tendency is to either ignore or criticize discouraged people. Without encouragement, the discouraged person starts to doubt themselves and become fearful. Before you know it, the poor soul is three-quarters of the way to defeat. Leaders are responsible for encouragement. If employees are expressing the firm has a negative work environment, it is a leadership, not a rank and file, problem.

The late teaching pro, Harvey Penick, once wrote, "If there is doubt in your mind … how can [you] know what [your muscles] are expected to do?"[8] While it is important to address shortcomings, building others up—which is my definition of encouragement—is more often the best way to help others. How often is the shortcoming I see so clearly in others the major flaw in my own life?

Be wary of an aspirant who either ignores mistakes or is quick to criticize others. Instead, be on the lookout for a person who enjoys encouraging others. While it is possible to train a person to develop a good work ethic, converting a discourager into an encourager is a tall order. It might be possible, but in my experience, it is rare. Discouragers are weights who sink ships, not raise them. Personally, people who discourage, ridicule, and hurt other people are not welcome in my world.

Encouragers come alongside other people and speak well to them. The Greek word for encourage is *parakaleo,* a compound word from para (to come beside) and kaleo (to speak well of). Everyone has a history, some of us more than others. Encouragers do not come alongside and *beat* people up. They come alongside and *build* people up. The last thing anyone needs is someone to remind them of how bad they are doing.

While there are numerous positive attributes of encouragers, these are ubiquitous character traits amongst them.

- **They are loyal.**
- **They do not allow disagreement to implode a relationship.**
- **They speak truth into people's lives.**
- **They listen and hear others empathetically.**

Dr. Daniel Goleman wrote two amazing books, *Social Intelligence: The New Science of Human Relationships* and *Focus: The Hidden Driver of Excellence.* In these books, he explains how heightened prefrontal activity in the brain associated with positivity enhances the ability to think creatively, maximizes cognitive flexibility, and allows the brain to process information more effectively. The left prefrontal area of the brain, Goleman writes, becomes extremely active (he calls it lighting up with activity when a brain is scanned) when we are in a positive state of mind.

In *Social Intelligence*, he discusses an experiment where the emotional tone of the leader in delivering a bad outcome made more impact than the news itself! He found when people were encouraging in delivering bad news, the receiver of the bad news said the interaction was positive. On the other hand, when good news was delivered in a discouraging or underappreciated fashion, the receiver of the news would describe the interaction negatively.

He contends employees remember negative interactions more than positive ones, which tend to spread negativity in the workplace.[9]

A caring leader has become such an exception to the rule that a person of encouragement stands out in a crowd like a beacon shining from a lighthouse. If I had to pick one trait I would insist on in a candidate, it would be a spirit of encouragement. Find people of encouragement, and you can train them to do most everything else.

Acceptance

Without a positive attitude, it is impossible to achieve a maximum level of success. It does not matter how hard you try—it simply will not happen.

Napoleon Hill, in his classic book, *Think and Grow Rich,* wrote, "The starting point of all achievement is desire." Indeed, your desire ultimately determines your destiny. "Weak desire," Hill said, "brings weak results as surely as a small amount of fire brings a small amount of heat."[10] Therefore, if you find yourself becoming negative, the remedy is to build a stronger fire under your desires because your attitude, not your aptitude, ultimately determines your altitude of success. Look, I am not trying to sound like Norman Vincent Peale. While it is essential for leaders to have skills, training, and experience, I will take someone with little experience and a great attitude over someone with great experience and a lousy attitude every single time.

"The key to maintaining a great attitude and positive spirit is to accept the things you cannot change."

The key to maximum success is the ability to adapt when things change. Sometimes things do not go as planned. Mike Tyson once famously said, "Everybody has a plan until they get punched in the mouth." What happens when things just do not go your way? You have done everything you are supposed to do, but it simply does not work out. What happens then? The key to maintaining a great attitude and positive spirit is to accept the things you cannot change.

Allow me to illustrate with a story.

Gary Player is one of the greatest golfers of all time, a GOAT as surely as Nicklaus or Woods. He was the third player in history, and only one in five to win all four of golf's major titles in his career. Player has won nearly 170 professional golf tournaments across every continent except Antarctica,[11] and was the first international player to win the coveted Master's green jacket. In the first round of the 1968 British Open, in Carnoustie, Scotland, the weather was not conducive to playing golf. It was freezing, and the wind chill from the 30+ mph wind made it feel worse. The best players in the world were being beaten up, and scores were skyrocketing. On the first tee, Gary Player said to his caddie, "Laddie, this is our kind of weather. We have a big advantage. I won my first British Open in weather worse than this." The caddie, concerned about the conditions, was extremely encouraged by Mr. Player's optimism. No one bettered 70 strokes on day one, and Gary was only four back in the wicked conditions.

The next day, the weather cleared, and the wind calmed. Player smiled at the beautiful day and said to his caddie, "Laddie, I love it when it is bright and beautiful. In these conditions, we are the ones to beat!" His caddie was confused but did not say anything. After a marvelous second round and on the heels of the leader, the caddie said to Player, "Gary, I am confused. On Thursday, you said you loved the wind. Today, you love the calm. Which is it, Gary? Do you love the wind or the calm?"

Gary smiled and said, "I love them both, Laddie. I have learned to not only accept the things I cannot change, but to *love* what cannot be changed."

Two days later, Mr. Player claimed his second British Open title when the wind (figuratively) blew most players away.

Do not confuse Gary's acceptance with apathy. Apathetic people are indifferent, complacent, and the first to quit. The Gary Players of the world, on the other hand, accept the things beyond their control. To them, tough breaks come with the territory. Sometimes the sure thing becomes the worst thing. Acceptance is an act of the will, a volitional choice. Apathy is a state of the heart—an emotional choice based on feelings, not fact.

Do you remember Charles Lindbergh, the aviation pioneer? Lindbergh was the first person to fly an airplane solo, the Spirit of St. Louis, across the Atlantic Ocean in 1927.

What about Bert Hinkler? Without Googling his name, few recall Hinkler was the *second* person to fly solo across the Atlantic. By all rights, everyone should know Hinkler and Lindbergh should be the afterthought. Hinkler was the best pilot of his day. His plane was the fastest on earth at the time. When he made his crossing, just a week after Lindbergh, his plane consumed less fuel. He cut six hours off Lindbergh's time and flew all the way to Latvia. In every way, save one, his was the better flight. Yet, when he arrived in Latvia, far beyond Paris, where Lindbergh had flown, no one other than the Latvians paid any attention. The press corps had already gone home. No one cared. He did it second. Who cares if his flight was *better*? History only cared about the fellow who did it first.

Ironically, Hinkler was prepared to leave the same night Lindbergh made his historic flight. The weather was bad, so Hinkler decided to wait. Lindbergh decided to take the Spirit of St. Louis up when Hinkler was unwilling to risk it. Lindbergh was not the better pilot. His was not the best equipment. Hinkler demonstrated as much the following week. Still,

Lindbergh flew when Hinkler did not. Lindbergh risked everything. Hinkler did not. Into a driving rain, and in fog so thick he had to fly 20 feet off the coast just to see where he was going, Lindbergh left as Hinkler hunkered down. History was made. Lindbergh was immortalized.

Do not misunderstand. The importance of talent, good equipment, and a top-notch plan are unequivocal. Certainly, both Lindbergh and Hinkler had all the prerequisites. Yet, it was Lindbergh's vision and his willingness to risk failure that separated him from his rival. Most entrepreneurs are exceptionally talented and offer great products and services. Certainly, talent has taken them to where they are today. However, being first requires more than talent and good products. It takes commitment to a vision and an acceptance of what cannot be changed. The weather was awful ... but Lindbergh flew anyway.

Hinkler made a decision that kept him out of the American history books. His decision not to fret about it led to another decision which immortalized him in Australia. In 1928, Hinkler made the first solo flight from England to Australia. It took him 15 days. Being an Australian, the country lauded his accomplishment and awarded him its highest honor, the Australian Air Force Cross. Hinkler accepted what he could not change. Lindbergh made the transcontinental flight first. Hinkler would attempt things Lindbergh never even considered. Tragically, in 1933, Hinkler was killed when his plane crashed in Italy after leaving Britain in what became a vain attempt to circumnavigate the globe. Hinkler was a man without fear or pretension. He may well have been the greatest pioneering pilot of all time. Accepting what you cannot change makes you decide to fly from London to Sydney after someone beats you across the Atlantic.

You will know you have found a potential Joshua when the things they cannot change do not hijack their attitude. I have had the pleasure of watching my colleague and successor, Mags, handle significant challenges with an attitude of acceptance worth envying. He still cannot use a screwdriver, but we have accepted that.

Tenacity

Back in the late 1990s, Greg Owen, a colleague in Australia, visited our home in Florida. Just before he came, I hired a new associate. My new hire was anxious to meet my Australian friend. The next morning, he was there bright and early to meet the man from *Down Under*. After the formalities, my young associate asked, "Greg, what is the secret to making it in the business?"

Greg thought a minute, and finally, he said, "Never quit."

"That's it?"

"That's it," Greg told him. "If you have not quit, you have not failed."

My associate never forgot those simple but profound words. He has not quit, and he is an amazing advisor to this day. He made it. He never quit. The advice Greg gave my young colleague is the most important thing a young person can hear.

"Be tenacious, because it is always too early to quit."

Earlier, I shared the story of Winston Churchill's address to his boyhood school of Harrow, where he stated succinctly, "Never, never, never, never give in." His message to these young gentries was simple: Be tenacious, because it is always too early to quit.

One of my favorite stories about tenacity culminated during the 2002 Winter Olympics. Steven Bradbury, a member of the Australian Speed

Skating team, was one of the best speed skaters of his time. He was also one of the least fortunate. Bradbury broke on to the world stage in 1991, when, at the tender age of 18, he was part of the Australian quartet who won the 5,000-meter relay in the World Championships in Sydney. It was the first time Australia had ever won a World Championship medal in a winter sport of any kind, and Bradbury was dubbed the next great speed skater in short track.

In 1994, during the World Cup in Montreal, another skater's blade sliced through Bradbury's right thigh after a collision. The skate cut through to the bone, and he lost an estimated four liters of blood. Bradbury's heart rate was nearing 200 bpm at the end of the race, and blood was everywhere. A quick-thinking doctor rushed out on the ice and saved his life by putting a makeshift tourniquet on the wound. All four of his quadriceps had been sliced, and Bradbury thought if he lost consciousness, he would surely die. He needed 111 stitches and could not move for 3 weeks. It took him 18 months to return to the strength necessary to compete again ... *but he refused to quit.*

He qualified for the 1998 Winter Olympics and was a sure medal contender. However, crashes impeded him in both the 500- and 1000-meter races, and he never made it out of the preliminaries. He could not believe his bad fortune ... *but he refused to quit.*

In September 2000, it appeared Bradbury's career was over when he broke his C4 and C5 vertebrae in a training accident. He spent a month and a half in a halo brace and needed four pins to be inserted in his skull and screws and plates bolted into his back and chest. Doctors told Bradbury that he would not skate again. Bradbury had other ideas. He was determined to reach another Olympics. He wanted redemption after the crashes in the individual races in 1994 and 1998. He conceded he was past his prime in terms of challenging for medals ... *but he refused to quit.*

Remarkably, Steven qualified for the 2002 Olympics in Salt Lake City in his specialty, the 1,000-meter short track event. He won his first heat convincingly, and it appeared his comeback would fall short when he placed third in the quarterfinals and only the top two from each heat advanced. However, the Canadian racer was disqualified, and Steven was awarded a spot in the semis. In the semifinals, Steven decided he would try a radical strategy and stay well back of the other skaters and hope for a crash, since all of his fellow competitors could outpace him. Sure enough, in the semifinals, three of the four ahead of him tangled on the last lap, crashed, and Steven sailed to a second-place finish, and a spot in the finals.

In the finals, Bradbury decided to try the strategy again. On the last lap, he was well behind his fellow competitors. All four racers out in front of him were cruising along and suddenly, they all crashed! Can you believe that? They were in the final corner, jostling for gold, and they *all* crashed. Bradbury avoided the pileup and cruised across the finish line to take the gold medal! He raised his hands in complete disbelief and amazement. He had become the first Australian to win a gold medal at a Winter Olympics event in *any* sport! The Australian Postal Service celebrated the event by putting his likeness on the 45-cent postage stamp. Steven was quoted after his victory as saying he would take the victory, not for the 90 seconds it took to win the race, but for the "last decade of the hard slog I put in."

Bradbury refused to quit, regardless of the tumult in his past. Tenacity means to stick like glue. To be tenacious requires living in the present, setting your sights high, and refusing to listen to your critics. Tenacity is at the heart of a great work ethic. The tenacious have ravenous fans encouraging them along the way. Tenacious leaders and competitors accept what they cannot change. They refuse to quit! Steven Bradbury is a wonderful example of what you are looking for in a successor.

Now go out and find a Joshua who is not afraid of a little SWEAT!

CHAPTER 7

THE FIVE
MUSTS OF SUCCESSION

If there are two chapters in this book you should read twice, it is this chapter and the next. Many people think absolutes are a myth—everything is relative—but *that* is the real myth. There have always been, and there will always be, certain inalienable truths. While there are many things business owners must do to be successful, there are at least five things every business owner needs to do if they want an effective transition from owner to successor and one thing you must avoid at all costs.

The Five Must-Dos of Succession

The jump from this generation to the next is usually difficult and often complicated. These five "musts" are essential to making your succession plan the success you hope it will be.

1. The candidate must be a *bona fide* candidate, or you are wasting your time.
2. The candidate must have the *It Factor*.

3. The candidate must be *integrated into the firm before taking over*.

4. The founder must play to the candidate's strengths.

5. The candidate must lead before becoming *The Leader*.

As I said above, there is also one *must not*, but let's save that for the following chapter.

For the most part, the advice of this chapter could have been written from the beginning of time. Absolutes are not subject to the winds of change—they are, well, absolute, or inalienable. Take this word of advice—ignore these *musts* and the *must not* at your peril!

Lessons from a Bedouin Shepherd

My wife and I have been fortunate to have spent some time visiting Israel. One day, we were heading down the road to visit Masada, and on the right-hand side of the road was a Bedouin shepherd with 100 or more sheep walking in the same direction along the side of the road. As our van sped by the shepherd and his flock, I turned to our guide and said, "That's amazing!"

He looked back with an incredulous look on his face. "What is amazing?"

"I am amazed the shepherd feels comfortable walking with a flock of sheep this close to a highway," I replied. "The sheep must be hit by vehicles all the time."

"Occasionally, but it is rare."

He then went on to give me a short education in sheep and shepherding. "The sheep completely trust their shepherd," he said. "People think sheep are stupid. However, sheep are some of the smartest animals on earth. Every sheep has a name, known only to the shepherd. The sheep knows their shepherd's voice and listens exclusively to him. If another person calls them, they will ignore the other voice. They do not pay any attention to a stranger because they do not know the stranger's intention. Their loyalty is tied to their shepherd. Most important, shepherds *lead* their flock. They do not *drive* their flocks."

I found the whole conversation fascinating. I was especially intrigued by his last statement, and I asked him to explain. "In America, you are famous for your cowboys. Cowboys drive cattle from one place to another. Shepherds lead. They never force the sheep in a direction. The shepherds lead their flock, and the sheep follow them because they trust the shepherd completely. Cowboys drive the cattle from behind and on their flanks. Shepherds stay in front of their flocks. Unlike the cowboys, shepherds do not yell. He simply starts moving, and the sheep follow. A shepherd never walks behind their sheep. He always walks ahead of them, and the sheep trust him implicitly.

"Because they know and trust his voice—and ignore every other voice—if the shepherd does not walk on the highway, neither will the sheep. They instinctively desire to remain safe. They feel protected in the flock and believe the shepherd will provide safe passage. Sheep are very reluctant to leave what they know and are naturally fearful. They rely heavily on their vision rather than their sense of smell. They see the shepherd taking the lead, and their fear of being left behind actually keeps them safe. Sheep are the most fascinating animals in the world."

His love for the Bedouin culture was captivating, and his words had such a profound effect on me. Indeed, I remember the conversation like it was yesterday, even though it occurred decades ago! As we arrived at our destination, he turned and said, "There are three things about sheep most people do not know. First, if they are caught, they would rather submit than rebel. Second, if they are lovingly handed over to a new shepherd, especially if they are not separated from their flock, they will begin following the new shepherd seamlessly. Finally, most people are sheep; very few are shepherds." With that, he turned and went to work, leading the *sheep* who were exiting the van.

> *"Most people are sheep; very few are shepherds."*

I remember a great deal about Israel, and this one conversation particularly. Over the decades since our conversation, I have thought about our guide's words deeply—especially his last few words: Most people are sheep; very few are shepherds.

The role of a financial advisor is akin to shepherding. For the most part, clients are incredibly smart followers looking for someone to trust. They want to be led, rather than driven to a decision. When they find a trustworthy shepherd, they pay attention when the shepherd speaks. Their natural desire is to trust a shepherd and follow the shepherd's direction. They are looking for guidance, not someone wielding a cattle prod, driving them from behind to keep moving. They want someone who will settle their fears and make them feel safe. They are reluctant to leave what they know, but if handed off to another shepherd lovingly, they are highly likely to seamlessly follow the new shepherd rather than bolt off to another one.

The lesson I took then, and share again now, is clients trust their advisors to look out for their best interest. This is never truer than when we are asking them to trust our selection of a successor. Clients need to be confident the person taking over can continue to settle their fears and make them feel safe. Since they are naturally reluctant to leave what they know, they will bolt in an instant if they believe the new shepherd is not the right person for them.

With this in mind, let's look at the *Five Musts* of succession.

1. The Candidate Must Be a Bona Fide Candidate

First and foremost, the candidate must be a *bona fide* candidate to succeed the founder. I define a bona fide candidate as someone the firm's key people, including the founder, would want as *their* shepherd. While many parents would love to see their children continue in their footsteps, is their son or daughter a bona fide candidate? Is the founder prepared to be their first client? If the answer is "absolutely!"—you might have a bona fide candidate. By the same token, if the answer is "I would, or could, if they had more knowledge and experience," you might have a bona fide candidate in the making. Bona fide candidates need to not only check the boxes we outlined in the last chapter in the acronym SWEAT, they must also have the desire, talent, and aptitude to lead the enterprise.

Our two children, Sydney and Reagan, are two of the smartest and most capable people I have ever met. Yes, I am biased, but I know I have two of the good ones. I am confident they will one day be extremely successful. Notwithstanding, right now, they are not bona fide succession candidates. First, they lack the desire to follow in their father's

> *"Lack of desire is always the preeminent disqualifier."*

footsteps. This could change, but as of this writing, they have seen the job and they do not want it! Lack of desire is always the preeminent disqualifier.

It is incredibly important to find out if your children's dreams align with yours. As we stand today, our children's dreams do not include financial services, and I refuse to force them into doing what they are not passionate about pursuing.

Only a few people can shepherd because it is a calling more than it is a job. As a result, not everyone is a bona fide candidate to succeed a founder. While everyone has different temperaments, choosing a candidate based on temperament is not a valid metric. Regardless of temperament, if a candidate lacks the SWEAT traits, go in a different direction. Furthermore, even if they possess those traits but lack the desire, talent, or aptitude to lead the enterprise, run in a different direction. However, take your time because determining whether a person has these traits and abilities does not happen overnight.

The Problem when Succession Is Unilateral

I have a close friend who was part of a third-generation family business in western Minnesota. His grandfather, originally a banker, lost his job during the Depression and began working on a local farm. While on the farm, he discovered farmers were paid to allow telephone lines across their property.

Around the turn of the 20th century, the independent telephone industry was starting to develop throughout rural America. The industry recruited farmers to build telephone systems on a cooperative basis. By 1929, when the Great Depression hit, there were about 6,000 mutual telephone systems strewn about rural America. The depression caused the industry to fall on extraordinarily hard times. The systems began deteriorating. Few subscribers paid their bills. Maintenance was spotty and telephone service was, to say the least, unreliable throughout rural America.

My friend's grandfather saw an opportunity most ignored. He believed telephones would one day be indispensable. Just before World War II, he obtained the rights to a telephone cooperative spanning several counties in his native western Minnesota. Both of his sons served in the military during the war. When they returned, their father, with the help of federal subsidies and a ton of hard work, had established a functional telephone system in western Minnesota—basically in the middle of nowhere! Both of his sons had the desire, talent, aptitude, and SWEAT necessary to lead the business. When they returned from active military service, they became an integral part of the enterprise. Their father diligently groomed the boys to succeed him. When he was ready to retire, both sons were prepared to assume leadership and had proven they were bona fide candidates to succeed their father.

By the late 1970s, the two sons of the founder, who each had two sons of their own, brought the four boys into the business. As my friend, who was one of the four, told me, even though his grandfather diligently prepared his sons to assume control, their fathers just assumed the grandsons would take over when they were ready to retire. They never had a written succession plan. It was just understood. The four boys would take over as their fathers had, regardless of the prerequisite desire, talent, aptitude, and SWEAT required to lead a 50-year old company. By this time, everyone had private lines in lieu of the party lines the customers used to share with their neighbors. Instead of a growth business, where they were always adding customers and expanding service, it had become a recurring revenue business focused on maintenance and improved quality of service.

In the early 1980s, both fathers (the sons of the founder) decided, without any significant discussion, it was time the company needed to be taken over by the four boys. They unilaterally transferred half of the shares of the company to the four sons, and their parents retained the other half. The boys were not asked to pay for the shares. One day they were employees, and the next, they were owners. However, within a short period of time, it became obvious there were problems. Unlike their grandfather, who had mentored his sons and groomed them to take over, the two sons had not done the same with their children. As my friend put it, "There were now four chiefs without any idea how to be chiefs leading a tribe who did not know who was in charge."

The 1980s ushered in a new era in the telephone business. In 1982, a landmark court ruling required AT&T to divest itself of its 22 Bell operating companies. Competition became fierce. Rural phone companies began expanding into cellular, cable TV, and even satellite communications.

Suddenly, instead of a mature company merely maintaining phone lines and making monthly collections, the industry had radically changed. The four grandchildren were faced with new decisions they were unprepared to make, but necessary to position the company for the future. Fortuitously, other rural telephone companies were looking to merge and acquire other competitors. They were approached by another cooperative looking to purchase the company and were able to sell it.

> *"If you are looking to have a child succeed you, would you have your son or daughter take over if he or she were not your child?"*

If you are looking to have a child succeed you, would you have your son or daughter take over if he or she were not your child? Lacking the desire, talent, and aptitude to lead the business, it became self-evident the four grandsons were never bona fide candidates to succeed their fathers. Absent the other cooperative buying them out, they could have easily ended up with little to show for the hard work and ingenuity of their grandfather.

Just Ask

John is a successful nephrologist. From the time his son, Randy, was a teenager, he loved medicine and only wanted to become a doctor. Randy graduated magna cum laude from a prestigious university and had his pick of medical schools. He graduated medical school at the top of his class. During his internship and residency, he decided to emulate his father and became a nephrologist. Even though he could have joined any number of practices around the country, he chose to join his father.

John could not have been prouder of his son. He was continually impressed by Randy's intuitive grasp of the specialty. John became excited by the prospect of his son succeeding him one day. Over time, John gave shares of the company to Randy in preparation for his son buying his interest entirely in the future.

One day, John asked his son about succession. Without hesitation, Randy said he was ambivalent to the business side of medicine and had neither the desire nor the aptitude for running the practice. He told his father while he loves treating patients, he has no interest in operations, which, coincidentally, is a passion of his father. To their credit, they mutually concluded Randy should practice medicine, and they would ultimately find another solution for running the practice.

They eventually merged with and sold their respective interests to another nephrology group. The merger allowed them both to be paid for the full value of the practice and continue to work as nephrologists. The merger gave John the opportunity to practice on a reduced basis and provided an excellent exit strategy. It also allowed Randy to do what he loves—treat patients—while someone else takes care of the *business of the business*. Even though Randy clearly has the desire, talent, and aptitude to be a great nephrologist, he does not have a desire to run the practice. As such, he is not a bona fide candidate to succeed his father.

2. The Candidate Must Have the *It Factor*

Every bona fide successor must possess the "It Factor," or what I call *The Factor*. Some people think *The Factor* is a God-given trait inherited by a select few, lucky enough to be born with it. Nonsense! The Factor is learned. No one is born with it! The problem is, most people have no idea what *it* is. They ramble on about how they cannot define it, but they know it when they see it. Balderdash!

The Factor is gained by learning specific behaviors. It is not an instinctive, natural gift granted to a select few by The Almighty. On the contrary, the behavior of those with The Factor is *learned*.

People with The Factor:

- Have charisma.
- Are confident without arrogance.
- Exude humility without humiliating others.
- Make others feel special.
- Are great storytellers.
- Are authentic—their rhetoric is congruent with their reality.

First and foremost, they have charisma, personified by grace. The Greek word for grace is *charis,* the root of charisma. Charisma is the ability to *influence people without force*. It is the primary trait of shepherds. Shepherds lead with charisma. John Maxwell wrote, "All leadership is influence, nothing more, nothing less."[1] People with charisma are influencers. They get people to move, much like shepherds with their sheep.

Second, they are confident, yet not arrogant. People with The Factor know their area of expertise inside out, yet they do not need to impress people. This is another aspect of grace. Rather than needing to impress, they are looking to be impressed.

People with The Factor exude humility—without humiliating others. They are comfortable in their own skin. In other words, they have learned to be comfortable with themselves.

Closely tied to confidence is the ability to make others feel special. When people with The Factor leave a meeting, people are apt to say, "I really love working with them." One way those with The Factor make people feel special is by being able to share a narrative that explains their idea. They are great storytellers comfortable explaining their point with a story.

Lastly, those with The Factor are authentic. Their rhetoric, what they say, is congruent with their reality, what they do. They say what they mean, and they mean what they say. This allows them to be persuasive while not overbearing. They would rather smile than frown; be assertive, yet friendly; driven, yet leading, not driving others.

Every one of these characteristics can be learned. They are not necessarily *God-given*!

Here is the secret to the *It Factor*—put others first. This is the sum of it all! Those who have it can teach it. Those who do not have it can learn it by putting others' needs above their own.

3. The Candidate Must Become Integrated Into the Firm

Even if you have a bona fide candidate, when is it the right time to throw them the keys? In our business, it took several years before it was obvious Mags was a bona fide successor candidate. However, like Dr. Randy, he had no interest in the business of the business either. If this is the case in your business, do not be deterred. Like my nephrologist friend, it became evident we needed a team to effectively accomplish our business continuity plan. Yet even after I was sure, it was five years until it was finalized. The message is this: **Start early!** It is highly likely it may take longer than you think before the candidate(s) are fully integrated into the fabric of the firm and ready to take over.

"Start early!"

Nevertheless, the candidate must be integrated into the firm before the deal is completed.

Integration is often more difficult but can be especially helpful when the successor is an outside buyer. While it may not be possible for an extended dating process, working together for a period before money changes hands can often lead to a successful merger and a better exit strategy. While Mags worked with us for a long time before we decided he was the right successor, the same was not true for Chad. To integrate Chad into the firm before taking over, we entered into a management agreement with each other. This gave each of us time to make sure the merger was right for both teams. After working together for two years, we were able to integrate and it cemented the merger. When I exited, there was no fuss, no muss. Once the right people are in place, make sure everyone is fully integrated before you toss them the keys to the kingdom.

Numerous businesspeople who saw their child as a bona fide succession candidate had their son or daughter work for a competitor with the intent to learn the business for several years before joining their firm. The key is it takes more than education to prepare a person for succession. A person will never know if they have the desire, talent, and aptitude for succession until they have survived the cauldron of the real world and have had their rear handed to them a few times.

One big mistake many parents make is promoting their child into the company's inner circle before the kid earns it. Every company has an inner circle of leadership. Depending on the size of the firm, it might be just two or three people, or it may be many more. Promoting an untested, unqualified person into a leadership role sends the wrong message to the key people and could easily undermine your son or daughter's credibility with clients and staff. Should the consensus within the firm become the candidate was promoted too soon, or only because they are the boss's son or daughter, their credibility may never recover. There is nothing wrong with a candidate starting at the bottom and working their way up. Wait until their integration is obvious to everyone else before elevating them. That said, let it happen organically. It will be good for the company and the candidate.

Timing is akin to riding a horse. I love what George Morris, the famed jumping instructor and competitor, was quoted as saying at a riding conference. "Imagine you are a horse. The most important [thing] from the horse's point of view is the way the rider communicates with the horse's mouth. Horse reins are not to be grabbed, leaned on, yanked, or pulled," Morris said. "They are a line of communication between [rider and horse]. When riders hold the reins incorrectly, they end up losing connection with [the] horse and [too often] punishing their mounts unintentionally."[2] The same can be said of when to toss the keys. Hold the reins tight enough to move the horse, but not so tight as to lose the connection or punish the business unintentionally.

The balancing act is to not be too soon nor too late. Indeed, waiting too long is often more harmful than leaving too soon. The hardest thing for many entrepreneurs is to let go. However, be confident in your decision-making. If you are fortunate, you will end up, like Goldilocks, with a porridge that is neither too hot, nor too cold, but "just right."

Four months after turning the business over to Mags and Chad, the world exploded, and we found ourselves in the middle of a pandemic! Some founders might have jumped back in and tried to "save the day." It might have been easy to justify such a decision. In our case, it would have been a major mistake. The pandemic forced Steve and Chad to lead. From time to time, they sought counsel, but they neither wanted, nor needed, a savior.

4. The Founder Must Play
To the Candidate's Strengths

Founders must focus on a candidate's strengths and surround them with a team whose strengths overcome the candidate's weaknesses. In 2005, the Harvard Business Review published a report entitled, "How to Play to your Strengths." In this report, they concluded "focusing on [the] problem areas [of others] prevents companies from reaping the best performance from people. Why should a natural third baseman labor to develop his skills as a right fielder?" Rather, the report resolved, we should, "Foster excellence in the third baseman by identifying and harnessing his unique strengths. It is a paradox of human psychology that while people remember criticism, they *respond* to praise. The former makes them defensive and therefore unlikely to change, while the latter produces confidence and the desire to perform better. Managers who build up their strengths can reach their highest potential. This positive approach does not pretend to ignore or deny the problems that traditional feedback mechanisms identify. Rather, it offers a separate and unique feedback experience that counterbalances negative input. It allows managers to tap into strengths they may or may not be aware of and so contribute more to their organizations."[3]

Mike Schmidt was perhaps the best third baseman in the history of Major League Baseball. Not only was he a juggernaut of a hitter, leading the National League in home runs 8 times, his defensive skills were easily as good as his offense as he was voted the best defensive third baseman 10 times over the course of his 19-year career. His 10 Gold Glove awards[4] are the most by any third baseman in Major League Baseball history. His combined offensive and defensive skills as a third baseman are what made him a first-ballot Hall of Fame selection and three-time National League Most Valuable Player. Thank goodness none of his managers thought he should have been a right fielder!

The more time leaders spend trying to make people strengthen their weaknesses, the less time they can spend playing to their strengths. Trying to get people to focus on fixing weaknesses they can delegate to someone else is unnecessary. It neglects what makes them appealing in the first place—their strengths. Worse, in the end, all they end up with is lost strength and strong weaknesses! We must always seek to find a way to develop Mike Schmidt into the best third baseman he can be. Support people's strengths and team them with others who are strong in the area they are weak. In other words, compliment your star third baseman by finding a star shortstop to play at his side!

Everyone has innate strengths and giftings. Exploit those strengths! If an aspirant is not detail-oriented, does it make sense to ask them to run the accounting department? John, my nephrologist friend, understood this intuitively. He recognized his son was a great practitioner who was not keen on running the business. His son's strength is treating kidney disease. John allowed his son to become a star kidney specialist and merged with another firm with a star-studded management team to manage the business. He could have tried to force his son to become a manager, but he wisely did not. Instead of asking Randy to become a mediocre businessman, he asked his son to become a Hall of Fame nephrologist. Randy focused on improving his strengths while others supported him in the areas Randy found a waste of his time.

My assistant, Kathy, was the first hire at our firm. In the beginning, it was Kathy and Don—a classic two-piece band. Kathy has mad administrative skills. She types about 1,000 words a minute (well, maybe a little less), remembers names and details like an iPhone, and generally knew what I needed before I realized I needed it—reminiscent of Donna on "Suits" or Radar from "M*A*S*H." Because of her awesome administrative talent, I presumed she would have a natural affinity for accounting. It turns out accounting is her kryptonite. While I was off galivanting, attempting to unearth the next great deal, she was totally overwhelmed with the task I had unceremoniously dumped in her lap.

One day, we received a notice from the Internal Revenue Service looking for quarterly tax withholding summaries of the company. She had no idea what she needed to do with the notice. She made the decision to put the letter in her desk drawer and discuss it with me the next day. Since I was on the road three to four days a week, office days were hectic and often exasperating for both of us. The next day, she completely forgot to discuss the notice in her drawer. Before long, a day turned into a week, then a month, then ... well, you get the idea.

The IRS does not have a great sense of humor, and this made them exceptionally unhappy. They sent a demand notice with substantial interest and penalties accrued. When the letter came, Kathy immediately called me. Suddenly the letter in her drawer went from important to urgent! She was in tears as she explained what had happened. The last thing I needed or expected was a problem with the IRS. Fortunately, I took the call in my car, which gave me a significant amount of time to mull over the situation. When I mentioned it to a colleague, he asked me, "Who are you going to hire to replace Kathy?" Even though it would have been easy to lay this on her, I was quickly reminded of something my mentor, Bruce Etherington, once said, "Problem, problem, who's got the problem?" This was not Kathy's problem—this was *my* problem.

> *"Problem, problem, who's got the problem?"*

I played to her weakness, not her strength. I was the one with the problem. I knew the taxes were due quarterly. I never examined whether they had been paid. In fact, I had never even asked her about the accounting. I assumed she was handling it in the remarkable way she handled everything else. When I returned, I went to Kathy and apologized. Had I been providing proper oversight, the event would have never happened. This became a watershed moment in our relationship. I am convinced we worked together for over 30 years *because* of this event, rather than despite it. It taught me one of the most important lessons I ever learned: You must put people in a position of strength. Just as importantly, always put people over profit. In the process of attempting to produce at a high level, I had neglected the most important asset I had—the other half of the two-man band. It also made me realize we needed a bigger band. We hired a great accountant and bookkeeper, more associates and support staff, and I never asked Kathy to play the outfield ever again.

Think of a business like a human body. Not everyone is the right hand, the left foot, or the heart. You do not ask the heart to walk, nor do you ask the right hand to pump blood through the veins within it. Every part of the body has a specific role. When all the parts of the body work together, the person can accomplish great things. When you place people in roles where they can excel, have faith they will excel, and let them excel!

5. The Candidate Must Lead Before Becoming *The Leader*

There is going to come a moment when it is time to toss the keys to the candidate and let them be the leader. Before you do, make sure they are ready to "drive the car" without you in the seat next to them. I will never forget the amazing experience I had teaching Sydney and Reagan to drive. They started by driving in the park at the end of our street. They made left and right turns, backed up, and learned to park the car properly. Once they were proficient in the confines of the park, they moved out to lightly traveled roads, until one day they were on the expressway. Ultimately, they were driving in rush hour traffic, having to make decisions on what to do when the unexpected happened. All the while, I sat in the passenger seat as they took turns behind the wheel. There were times it was a little nerve-racking, but after many hours of mentoring, it became evident they were ready. After passing their driver's test with flying colors, they soon began driving every day without Dad sitting next to them. I was confident they could handle whatever came their way—and if not, they know where I live.

In the same way, the successor candidate must be leading before becoming *The Leader*. The key staff knows if and how well the candidate leads. The staff also has an opinion as to whether the candidate is ready to lead. When long-time employees express concern over a candidate's readiness or ability to lead, listen to them! It is in their best interest to have your back. For the most part, key employees want the transition to work as much, if not more, than the founder does. If the successor candidate is not ready, there is a very real risk of losing key people when the founder exits. Do not overrule the company's inner circle! Make sure there is consensus within the leadership team the candidate is leading effectively long before they are The Leader.

Secondly, the founder should remain involved for a period after the baton has been passed. The worst thing a founder can do is toss a succession team the keys and move to Tahiti. Most successors need help for a while. The founder has vast knowledge and experience the successor does not have. Give the successor access to that knowledge and experience because no one knows what they do not know. It also allows for a smoother transition for the firm's clientele. Consider the shepherd example. Sheep are reluctant to leave what they know, but if handed off to another shepherd perspicaciously, sheep will seamlessly follow the new shepherd. Give clients and staff the time they need to get used to the new shepherd.

A founder being available to the successor is priceless. No matter how well a colleague is prepped to take over, there is always going to be something they are unprepared to tackle. Consider the founder remaining on the payroll for a while. In fact, it is a good idea to make the compensation paid a part of the purchase price. This move formalizes the founder's commitment to assist the successor as they take over. Allowing the founder to stay involved, on a diminishing basis, while allowing the successor to assume the boss' role is normally good for both parties. The founder can comfortably transition to the next stage of his or her life, while the successor becomes The Leader.

By the same token, the founder should not hang around too long. Be careful not to undermine the successor's authority. It is fine to come in occasionally to work on a project, but the founder's involvement should dwindle as the successor becomes more comfortable in the role.

Let the kids drive the car without Mom or Dad in the passenger seat. While it is true, an accident can (and probably will) happen, take the risk and trust the decision. Your successor and the business will be better for it.

Do not neglect these must-dos when it comes to succession. You must have a bona fide candidate with *The Factor*, who has fully integrated into the role and

> *"You must not make decisions based on fear."*

is playing to their strengths before they become *The Leader*. Trust your decision and never overrule your gut. The final "must" is the one must *not* on the list.

You must not make decisions based on fear.

CHAPTER 8

AND ... ONE MUST NOT

I f there is only one piece of advice a person could be given in life, it would be: Never make decisions based on fear!

Fear is the antithesis of trust. It instigates bad decisions and can paralyze people from deciding at all. Worse yet, fear, like quitting, can easily become a person's fallback position. If you do not know or understand something, do not trust either people or information, or think something may harm you, and the fallback position is fear, *look out!*

> *"Fear is the antithesis of trust."*

Fear is so common among people it has become an acceptable response to challenging circumstances. Society accepts the contention that it is customary to be afraid and thereby allows fear to be the normal response. The truth is when you allow fear to be an acceptable response to a challenging situation, the more apt you are to make fear your go-to response. When fear is acceptable, it is easy to become entangled in a cycle of fear. This cycle of fear typically starts with an event or situation that scares you. The situation becomes convoluted by a *fear trigger,* which in itself has little association with the facts of the event. Rather, fear imagines the worst possible outcome, only occasionally based on facts, but more often on a distortion of the truth. Fear frequently distorts a situation to the point where the fear becomes greater than the event itself. After the bombing of Pearl Harbor, President Franklin Roosevelt said it best, "The only thing we have to fear, is fear itself!"

COVID-19 is an excellent example. There is no doubt the coronavirus is a highly contagious, sometimes ravenous disease everyone should try to avoid. Nevertheless, some were so petrified by the virus they stopped living. While it is completely appropriate to do all you can to avoid contracting a virus, the fear of *becoming* infected can be equally perilous because it can lead to manufacturing ways that you *might* catch the disease, causing you to be afraid to leave your own home.

Fake Evidence Appearing Real

FEAR has been referred to by the acronym, ***Fake Evidence Appearing Real.*** Left unchecked, fear can take you to a place where your imagination kicks in, and you feel both out of control and out of your comfort zone. This is because fear finds its root in feelings rather than facts. What begins as a legitimate concern—a disruption, a disaster of sorts, an uncomfortable situation, something you do not understand or trust—suddenly morphs into something more dire because of fear.

The craziest part is fear can activate your nervous system, making what is not real *feel* physically real. This fear of what *might* happen causes the blood to drain from the pre-frontal cortex, the part of the brain responsible for emotional expression, problem-solving, memory, and judgment. Logic starts to disappear, clarity is lost, and thinking becomes confused. When a person makes decisions in this mental state, the chance of making the best decision becomes random, at best. Once the cycle of fear starts, it is extremely hard to break. This is not to say people like fear or *want* to be afraid—they just start fearing what might happen because it is their fallback position.

Breaking the Cycle of Fear

The only way to break the cycle of fear is through *knowledge*, leading to *faith*, leading to *trust*. The more you know about something, the less you will fear it, and the more you will start believing there is a better way to overcome the situation than by being afraid. Faith is believing there is a process capable of conquering the situation, eliminating fear, and solving the dilemma. Trust is putting that faith into action by committing to the process through a well-thought-out plan you believe will give you the best opportunity for a positive outcome. Hence the expression, *trust the process!*

Let me give you a simple example. Assume years ago, you sat in a wooden chair, and it did not hold your weight. It could have been poorly constructed, sabotaged, or any number of other

> *"Until you sit in the chair and risk an outcome, you remain in the cycle of fear."*

issues, but the bottom line is you sat in a wooden chair in the past, and it collapsed. You see another wooden chair. You refuse to sit in the chair because you fear, like the chair in the past, it will not hold your weight. To assuage your fear, an engineer comes along and says, "I will prove the chair is safe. Let's place these sacks of flour on the chair until the flour equates to your weight." Seeing the chair can hold the weight of the flour, the fear is mollified, and you believe the chair is safe—that is *faith*. Nevertheless, the cycle of fear of the chair collapsing is not broken until you *sit* in the chair—that is *trust*. No matter how much "faith" you have in the safety of the chair ... Until you sit in the chair and risk an outcome, you remain in the cycle of fear.

No one is exempt from being afraid. No one knows what is going to happen in the future. The only way to bridge the gap between fear and acceptance is to acknowledge the fear. Acknowledging what makes you afraid is the precursor of faith and ultimately trust. Going back to the chair example, until you acknowledge the fear of sitting in wooden chairs, the fear will not be mollified, and the cycle of fear remains intact. Once fear is acknowledged, you consider ways to determine the chair might be safe. However, only when you have the faith to actually sit in the chair can the cycle of fear be broken.

Faith is like a muscle. The more you exercise it, the stronger (and bigger) it becomes. It is easy to be afraid when your future is at stake, but faith is stronger than fear! By the same token, there is no need to be reckless.

One of my favorite jokes is, "What are the last words of a redneck?"

"Hold my beer and watch this."

When something frightens you, the first thing you need to do is stop, acknowledge the fear, get the facts straight, and determine what is making you afraid. Once you have acknowledged exactly what is causing you to be afraid and done everything you can to understand and protect yourself from your fear, the next step is to talk about it with someone who knows how to help you understand the truth, e.g., the engineer in our example above. Once you obtain reasonable counsel, have faith in the counsel, and determine the best process—what *can* be done—to overcome the fear. Then trust the process, regardless of the outcome. The outcome, unlike the process, is out of your control.

I have an older friend who became effectively incapacitated over a fear of falling. It started when, for no apparent reason, he fell. Every time he would go out, he believed he was going to fall. Pretty soon, he stopped going out. Because of his inactivity, his muscles started to atrophy, and he gained a significant amount of weight. The weight made him even more unstable. This significantly increased his actual risk of falling, leading to less activity, more tension, more fear, and physical pain eclipsing even the pain of falling. It was a classic example of the cycle of fear in action.

When Fear and Succession Are Imperfect Bedfellows

Jerry was a successful financial advisor in northern Florida. Despite his success, he grappled with fear. Sometimes his fear paralyzed him. Other times, fear precipitated irrational decisions preceding his "paralysis by analysis." As his fear grew, he would start overanalyzing everything. His fear of making a bad choice made him incapable of coming to difficult decisions. This inevitably frustrated his staff. Seeing the staff was frustrated, he would begin making rash choices he almost always regretted.

Jerry had thought about succession planning from time to time, but never seriously. He did not recruit, train, or develop people within or without the organization to succeed him. Jerry consistently operated reactively rather than proactively. He reactively chose to share an office with several different advisors over the years. A classic one-man band, he made no attempt to develop a team. It appeared nearly every time I saw him, he had another new staff member assisting him. Even the concept of being a member of a firm was foreign to him. Rather, he shared common space and split expenses with several other advisors.

Although he liked the other people in his office, he neither respected his peers nor saw any of them as worthy business partners or succession candidates. The other advisors were all about his age, and he was convinced they would most likely leave the business long before he did. The thought of any one of them having the financial capacity to buy his business seemed nonsensical. Besides, his plan was to work into perpetuity. Even though the stress of the business got to him at times, he did not have any interest or intention to retire—or even slow down. The truth was, his identity was wrapped up in his business—he was a financial advisor, nothing more and nothing less.

Just a few months short of his 65th birthday, Jerry was in Gainesville visiting a client within earshot of the University of Florida's world-renowned Shands Medical Center. Soon after arriving at his client's office, he became short of breath. Minutes later, he began to suffer a serious heart attack. His client recognized his symptoms, and his quick thinking to call 911 immediately saved Jerry's life. He was rushed to Shands Heart & Vascular Hospital, and within minutes he was on the surgical table of one of the leading cardiac care units in the country. His heart attack was massive and caused significant damage to his heart and vessels. He went from workaholic to incapacitated in the blink of an eye. The doctors later told his family they lost him on the table—not once, but *twice*. His prognosis was not good. After weeks in hospital, rehab, recuperative care, and therapy, he returned home, a shell of the man he once was.

To their credit, the advisors in his office rallied around Jerry. They watched over his clients and supported his beleaguered staff while he battled to recuperate. His wife came to the office every day to do what she could, but it was clear it was going to be a long time before Jerry would be able to return, if ever. His broker/dealer paid close attention to his medical condition and what was happening with his accounts. A few months into his ordeal, one of the advisors saw Jerry at his home. He recommended Jerry talk to a person he had met at a conference who was interested in purchasing other practices.

With each passing day, Jerry slipped further into a cycle of fear. He started to believe he would never completely recover. He feared the longer he was away, the less valuable his practice would become. He became convinced if there was a talented, younger producer out there in a financial position to buy him out, he had to consider it, but he was afraid. He had never planned for this and was afraid of losing everything he had built over this long career. Jerry knew he had to find someone quickly. He feared the other advisors would steal his clients, which was, by the way, completely unfounded and untrue. He was afraid if he waited too long, the business would quickly lose value. Most of all, he was not afraid, but *terrified,* by his incapacity.

He decided to talk to the young advisor his colleague recommended. Jerry and Charles, the young advisor Jerry's colleague recommended, spoke on the phone numerous times. Finally, they met face to face at Jerry's home. Charles liked Jerry and wanted to help him. He was extremely interested in buying his book of business. After significant due diligence, Charles made Jerry an offer to buy his book. After a bit of haggling, they came to a financial agreement... *with a caveat.* Should Jerry recover, Charles agreed to allow Jerry to come back and work with him in the future. Charles was excited to capture a new book of business in another locale, and never considered the ramifications of the caveat, so he agreed to it.

Meanwhile, Jerry's fear was nearly overwhelming him. How could this be happening? How could his health fail him? Mostly he feared a loss of his identity. He feared losing his will to live. He feared death.

Shortly after the sale closed, he suddenly began regretting his decision. He was convinced he could have made a better deal. Even though the deal was more than fair, Jerry could not shake the fear Charles had taken advantage of his ill health and structured a less than equitable agreement to purchase Jerry's business.[1] Fear had displaced reality. He was lost. He had allowed fake evidence not only to appear real, but to become his truth.

As part of the agreement, Jerry drafted a letter introducing Charles to his clients. The letter explained he had sold the business to Charles and expressed Jerry's ongoing concern for his clients and admiration of his successor. Charles began calling and meeting with clients as soon as the deal was closed and was pleased by the results. Jerry's clients were also pleased. They were excited for both Jerry and Charles. They were happy Jerry was being rewarded for selling his practice, and they were equally excited about the young advisor Jerry had, in their minds, handpicked.

About six months after his heart attack, Jerry's health suddenly started taking a turn for the better, and he began to improve significantly. About a year after the sale, Jerry declared he was completely recovered! He showed up at Charles' office with a message—he wanted to exercise his contractual caveat and return. By this time, Charles was doing a remarkable job with Jerry's clients and had nearly doubled the revenue being generated with Jerry's old clients from the prior year. Jerry thought Charles would be excited about having him back. He believed he could step back in and partner with Charles seamlessly.

Neither Charles nor Jerry were prepared for what was about to happen. There was no question in Jerry's mind that Charles had purchased the right to receive the residual income being generated by the work Charles was doing with Jerry's clientele. What Jerry did not understand was he was not entitled to meet with a former client and write new business with the client and be compensated. If he wanted to come back, he would have to develop all new contacts. Jerry was not allowed, by contract, to solicit business from his old clientele. Jerry was stunned. Charles, on the other hand, suddenly found himself in a contentious relationship with Jerry he never saw coming.

Unfortunately, this did not end well. Charles ultimately filed a lawsuit to keep Jerry from working with his old clients. It became very acrimonious. Even though Charles ultimately prevailed in mediation, the litigation cost him money, time, and significant extra work to protect his investment. Jerry's fear turned to anger, and, two years later, he died. I am convinced the stress caused by his fear and subsequent anger were key factors in Jerry's medical relapse. All the result of Jerry violating this one vital absolute: You must not make decisions based on fear!

Jerry never acknowledged his fear and was incapable of realizing fear had darkened his perception and made him incapable of seeing things as they really were. This clouded his judgment and created even more anxiety. On the flip side, had he acknowledged the fear, he would have had the opportunity to exercise faith and trust his decision.

> *"Just as light cannot coexist with darkness, neither can faith coexist with fear."*

Just as light cannot coexist with darkness, neither can faith coexist with fear. When light comes into a dark place, the darkness disappears. The same is true with faith and trust. Once fear has been acknowledged, faith and trust can replace the anxiety because they are the antithesis of fear and anxiety, and the antidote to the cycle of fear.

We all have a choice. We can either live in faith or in fear. I define faith as *believing what is true without an assurance of the outcome.* I remember watching a Tiger Woods interview after he won a big golf tournament. One putt had made all the difference. He said he examined the final putt with his caddie and determined what he needed to do to make the putt. He had complete faith if he hit it at a certain speed, on the line he chose, the putt would break a specific amount and go in the hole. Just before he was ready to hit it, doubt came creeping into his mind. He said he verbally scolded himself. He literally began yelling internally, "Trust it!" He reaffirmed his decision and trusted it. He stroked the putt on the chosen line, at the chosen speed, and the ball found the hole.

The Inward Cycle of Fear

As shared previously, you want a succession candidate with the attributes of SWEAT—Sight, Work, Encouragement, Acceptance, and Tenacity— along with the desire, talent, and aptitude to lead the enterprise. If a person possesses these qualities, they have a better than average chance of success. Did you notice that fear is *not* part of the traits necessary to succeed? Fear is always trying to poke its head in there, but when a person is building a great business, they do not have time to allow fear to shortcut the process. That does not mean fear is not busy attempting to interrupt it anyway. Every time fear sticks its head into the process to disrupt it, acknowledge the fear; do not ignore it! Do what Tiger did. Scold the fear and replace the anxiety with faith and trust the process. In my experience, the most debilitating fear comes *after* success, because then you have something to lose. When we are first getting started, we are like Mayo, the character in *An Officer and a Gentleman*—he had nothing to lose. However, as success grows, fear comes into your head, threatening to take it all away.

Everyone struggles with fear. It is as normal as breathing. The issue is, what do you do when fear starts rumbling in your head, and you cannot keep it away? It is important to rebuke fear early because left alone, the first thing fear does is **distract**. Fear does not care how successful you are, how important you think you are, or how good you are. No one is exempt from fear's attacks. Fear is agnostic. It does not discriminate. It could not care less about ethnicity, political beliefs, or religious convictions. Fear does not care who it attacks or attempts to destroy it. Its treachery is its subtlety. It begins its process of deceit by luring you into the snare of distraction. Fear starts by distracting you from what it takes to generate success or influence. This leads to worrying about inconsequential things instead of what really matters. Distraction is especially sinister because it is normally fed by ego. Suffice it to say, if you ignore fear's distractions early, you will pay for it later.

Distraction Leads to Drift

While you are distracted, fear begins to incubate. If left to its own devices, during its incubation, fear causes people to **drift**. Drifting is a painfully slow process of cleverly taking its subject off course. Anyone who has ever fished in a current knows the power of drift. If a boater is faced with a north current at two to four nautical miles per hour, like what Floridians face when they are offshore in the Gulf Stream, the only way to nullify drift is to move against it at a rate faster than the current. This is easy with a motor, but virtually impossible with an oar.

Of course, the easiest way to defeat drift is to never get distracted in the first place. When a leader is focused, there is no time to be either distracted or bored. Unfortunately, or maybe fortunately, we are humans, not Vulcans. Humans get bored. They get distracted. Occasionally, focus wanes. Nevertheless, when the distraction mutates to drift, the most common reaction is anxiety. Facing anxiety and the phobic cause, distraction, early and head-on, gets a person back on course relatively quickly. At this point, you can easily refocus, get back on course, and move on. On the other hand, inactivity and boredom feed anxiety ravenously. The less you exercise your unique abilities, the more it feeds distraction. The greater the distraction, the greater the drift. Drift, because it is slow and innocuous, is easy to ignore, but dangerous when you do.

Drift Leads to Doubt

Fear frequently causes leaders to forget what got them to where they are in the first place. They become distracted, begin to drift, and, if left unchecked, drift will lead to **doubt**. Overcoming the effects of doubt necessitates three different course corrections.

First, you need to refocus your time away from what is distracting you and get back to doing what got you to where you are in the first place. Do not let the distraction become your truth.

Focus on what you know to be true, not pretense. Remember, fear is *Fake Evidence Appearing Real.* Fear is fueled by fake evidence and ignores the truth.

> *"Do not let the distraction become your truth."*

Second, look fear in the face and speak it out of existence. My father was a big proponent of the expression, "Say it out loud!" When he would see one of us being overly quiet, he would say, "What's going on? Say it out loud!" This may sound strange, but you need to speak fear *into* existence before you can speak it *out* of existence. When you say things out loud, even when no one else is there, it allows you to see whether what you are thinking is truth or fear speaking lies, attempting to undo all you have previously done. It is amazing how impactful it is to express what you are thinking—*out loud*. I am not suggesting shouting from the rooftops. Rather, get alone, write down the things you are anxious about and read what you have written. **Say it out loud!** Without being metaphysical, do not be afraid to let fear hear the truth. Speak fear into existence, and you will be able to rebuke the fear. When you do, it will run and hide, because fear does not operate in the light. It lives and operates in the shadows of our subconscious.

Third, get back to work! Getting back to doing the things that made you successful in the first place will fight the distraction, drift, and doubt that fuel the fear. In fact, if you do not get back to work, you will inevitably remain in the cycle of fear and fall even deeper into fear's downward spiral. Hard work spurred your success in the first place. So, get back to work! Distraction pulls people away from what is important. It makes you think you are working when, in fact, you are just messing around. I remember Bud Jordan saying numerous times, "Go to the beach! At least then you will *know* you are not working."

The Insidious Nature of Doubt

Doubt is insidious and more devious than people imagine. It makes people anxious and steals away success, even amid the most profound achievements. In fact, it will do all it can to keep someone from succeeding.

In 2018, PGA Tour professional golfer Michael Kim was working hard to achieve his dream of succeeding on the PGA Tour. After an amazing college career, he turned pro in 2014 and immediately qualified for what was then known as the Web.com Tour, the developmental tour for professional golfers attempting to reach the PGA Tour. After two excellent seasons on the Web.com Tour, he qualified to play on the PGA Tour. Over the next three PGA Tour seasons, Michael's career steadily improved. He hit a pinnacle with a record-breaking eight-shot victory at the John Deere Classic in the middle of 2018.[2] Winning changed things for Michael. The victory made him exempt on Tour through 2020. It also gave him an invitation to play in the prestigious Open Championship in Great Britain the week after the John Deere event.

He played brilliantly at the Open. Even though he stumbled a bit on the last day, he finished a respectable 35th in a field of 156 of the world's greatest players. After he won, he decided if he was going to win consistently, he needed to change his game. He had just won a huge event in record fashion, and he thought he needed to change? With money in his pockets and his career secure for the next two years, he became distracted and quickly drifted from what made him great in the first place. He started making wholesale changes. He hired a new coach and attempted to revamp his swing. Before long, the things that had made him successful were being replaced with new ideas and different thoughts. He lost his edge, and drift turned to doubt. Suddenly, he went from one of the best professional players in the world to one of the worst. On the PGA Tour, except for rare exceptions, either 144 or 156 players play on Thursday and Friday for the right to play on

Saturday and Sunday. The top 65 players after Friday, including ties, make the *cut* and the balance of the players go home—without a paycheck. The PGA Tour is the ultimate form of capitalism!

After his win and a good week in Great Britain, the wheels fell off! He made only one cut over the remainder of 2018 after playing in the Open. In the calendar years 2019 and 2020, he missed **every** cut over a two-year period, lost his playing privileges, and is no longer active on the PGA Tour. Every time Michael had an opportunity to play the weekend, something would happen to bedevil him. I scoured the PGA Tour records looking for someone who struggled more after winning, and Michael is without peer. Sadly, when you listen to the interview he gave after he won, he spoke more about his fear of losing than he did about the thrill of winning.

In an interview in *Golfweek* a year after his win, and midway through his unprecedented collapse, he seemed overly focused on the two-year exemption he received for winning the tournament. Rather than trying to repeat what he did when he won, he said the exemption gave him the time he needed to work on changes in his swing with his new coach. The objective, he said, was "to have more weeks like I did at the Deere more consistently."

"It's taken a little longer than I hoped or wished, but it's kind of the ultimate one step back, to go two steps forward," Michael said. "I'm content with finding where my game is starting to head, and I'm excited for the second half [of the season]. Obviously, I'd like to play better, but looking at the latter half of this year and the upcoming year, I'm excited to see where my game will be." Unfortunately, it never came back, and today, he is essentially out of a job. Such is the insidious nature of doubt!

From Doubt to Denial

Doubt prohibits a person from performing at the highest level. Worse, doubt is a trust-killer. When our minds start to drift, the resulting doubt leads the mind to question even things it knows are true. When doubt becomes the preeminent force in our decision-making, we go from doubt to **denial**, and faith and trust are out the window. The fear-filled person begins to deny they are even in trouble. Read Michael Kim's comments again, and the denial is self-evident. He stopped believing in the process he used on the way up that led to his great success. He was sure he was just having a bit of a setback. He believed the lies and fake evidence fear had put in his head.

Denial is a legitimate way to help cope with a troubling situation on a temporary basis. Sometimes the only way to get through a horrible experience is to deny it for a time. Psychologists call it the *Denial Syndrome*. According to an article published by the Mayo Clinic, when you are in denial, you are "trying to protect yourself by refusing to accept the truth about something that's happening in your life. It is a mechanism that gives you time to adjust to distressing situations—but staying in denial can interfere with your ability to tackle challenges."[3] While denial can help short-term, staying in denial will not overcome the damage fear is causing.

Denial Leads to Being Dull of Hearing

When people start denying they are in trouble, they stop hearing those who can help them the most. They often stop seeking and receiving counsel and become what I call **dull of hearing**.

"When people start denying they are in trouble, they stop hearing those who can help them the most."

Becoming dull of hearing does not mean someone is deaf. It also does not mean they no longer seek counsel. It means they do not **believe** the counsel. They stop trusting what they hear, and they lose their faith in the process! While the single best way to crush fear is trusting the truth, those in denial reject the truth with prejudice. Fear paints lies as truth, and fear-based lies convolute the truth.

A person can live in fear or faith, but not both. Indeed, fear's primary charge is to break down faith. One of the sure signs of having fallen down the rabbit hole is you no longer trust the counsel of those who, heretofore, have never intentionally led you astray. When a person doubts the counsel of those who love and care about them the most, they are most likely spinning around in the cycle of fear.

The Final Vortex of Fear

When a person has allowed fear to grip their thinking to this extent, they are now a few steps away from the final vortex of fear—**departing** from and **despising** what they used to love. When fear takes root, it is hard to admit the truth ever existed in the first place. Fear has completed its work when the one in fear no longer trusts anything or anyone.

Fear is a treacherous beast prepared to swallow everything a person has built. Its greatest weapon is the downward cycle of fear that begins with:

- ➢ **Distraction**.
- ➢ Leading to **drift**.
- ➢ **Drift** leads to **doubt**.
- ➢ Leading to **denial**.
- ➢ **Denial** leads to being **dull of hearing**.
- ➢ Leading to **departing**.
- ➢ Which leads ultimately to **despising** what is good.

Do not give fear even the slightest opportunity. Avoid anxiety and refuse to make decisions based upon fear! While easier said than done, the weapon of our warfare against the beast of fear is faith. As I said earlier in the chapter, I define faith as *believing what is true without an assurance of the outcome*.

Trust It!

No one has any idea what the future holds. The future is meant to be scary, but the future is faced in the present. Fear wants us anxious about tomorrow and neglecting today. Every victory is won one shot at a time. Every battle is won in the present. Nothing can change what has happened in the past, but you can learn from it to impact the present and influence the future. Focus on what is happening right now and hold on to what you know is true.

Always trust what you know in your heart of hearts is true, even when fear is screaming, "You are a fool!" As Lin-Manuel Miranda wrote in his score of *Hamilton*, "I'm not throwing away my shot." Trust the process! Trust is a certain way to overcome anxiety and defeat the malevolence of fear. Do not let fear cause you to throw away your shot ... or fail to end with the beginning in mind.

CHAPTER 9

FAMILIAL SUCCESSION

It was Christmas Eve, and Sharon was sitting on the edge of her childhood bed. She knew she had to go to her grandmother's house to spend the holiday with her parents, aunts, uncles, brothers, sisters, cousins, nieces, and nephews. In fact, she was convinced half the county was somehow related to her. Her family was out of control. All she wanted to do was curl up in a ball and cry. The thought of having to face them was wearing her out! The last thing she wanted to do was tell her crazy family the latest happenings in her life. Certainly not after the events at lunch.

Her fiancé, Julian, had told her the marriage was off. The plan was to surprise everyone and introduce him to the family on Christmas Eve, but he was already on a plane back to Florida. When she arrived, she took her mom aside and said, "Please do not tell ANYONE. I beg of you; do not tell *anyone* we broke up."

Within minutes, her cousins, aunts, uncles—even her eight-year-old niece came over to express their condolences. Sharon grabbed her mom.

"Mom, I told you not to tell anyone!" she spouted off, enraged that her mom had gone against her word.

"I didn't tell anyone, Sharon. Just the family."

Family is different. You can pick your friends, but you cannot pick your family. After all, family is how many people discover the *fun* in dysfunction. Add familial succession into the mix, and things can get interesting, to say the least!

Fair—Not Equal

According to a report published by Massachusetts Mutual in 2018, nearly 60% of family business owners plan to split their companies equally between their children[1]. When you have a family business, leaving it to your children is far different than passing down an investment account or selling it to an outsider. Indeed, passing shares in a family enterprise to family members not actively involved in the company might be a recipe for enmity between those working for the company and those not actively involved, resulting in a poor outcome for all.

Fair does not necessarily mean equal. It is common for one sibling to have an aptitude and excitement for a family business and devote him- or herself to it, while another takes a different path. Is it fair to either of those siblings to expect them to take on equal ownership in the family business after their parents are no longer involved in the family company?

When a child works with his or her parents, and the other children choose different occupations, it is unrealistic to believe common ownership in family business will not be a spark setting aflame a disaster. Why? Because there is a major difference between ownership succession and management succession. Parents and heirs frequently mix these up. It is not uncommon for a parent to think something like, "Our daughter, who is working hard in the business, will be our management successor." Even though their son is an attorney in another state and has no interest in Dad's financial planning firm, the parents seem to think he and his sister can still manage as joint owners. Frankly, it is hard to imagine the daughter being delighted with the prospect of becoming a partner with her brother, who has never been even a *remote* part of the enterprise and is not interested in being involved in the future.

Whether transferring control to family members or non-family members, the more successful a company becomes, the more careful a founder must be in the transfer of ownership, especially when the transfer is to their adult children. Since every family, and business, is different, every situation requires a nuanced and unique approach to familial succession to avoid one child having nothing to do with his or her sibling again because one or more of the children feel Mom or Dad did not treat them fairly. Non-working family members can frequently feel they are *entitled* to something from the company, while the working sibling often resents this perceived entitlement. Suffice it to say, the conversation about who is going to either buy the shares of the firm or inherit them is a conversation every parent considering familial succession must have with their adult children. In the example above, the daughter may indeed end up with a greater monetary inheritance than her brother. There are ways to rectify the discrepancy. Life insurance payable to the son may be an option, but sometimes you need to accept that fair is not always equal.

The Need for an Arm's-Length Agreement

Another inherent problem in familial succession is the lack of a truly *arms-length succession agreement* between parent and child. To be clear, a transaction is considered at arm's length when both parties to the agreement are not acting against their own self-interest. In other words, the buyer—in this case, the child—is looking for the best deal for the child. Likewise, the seller—in this case, the parent—is similarly seeking the best outcome for the parent. When two parties are negotiating at arm's length, the result is a transaction at the *fair market value*, or the price any stranger would pay for the same asset under the same terms. When a seller conveys a business to a non-family member, the buyers and sellers have negotiated a price and terms acting primarily in their own separate interests. The parties work independently, without one party holding significant influence over the other. An arms-length transaction is usually not made under pressure or coercion. Indeed, both the buyer and the seller possess equivalent bargaining power and act to negotiate a deal that is in their own self-interest.

The same cannot always be said when a business is transitioning from a parent to a child. Short of both parents dying suddenly and simultaneously, it is rare a founder/parent makes a clean break from their company. Even though Mom or Dad may cease performing day-to-day operations, they often continue to exert considerable influence over their children. Many times, parents continue to maintain ownership and merely transfer the management responsibility to their adult children. Even though their adult children may have grown children of their own, it is often hard for Mom and Dad to stop wanting to wield their influence over both their children and the enterprise itself.

If Mom and Dad were selling the business to a non-family member, they would hire an attorney and negotiate an arm's-length contract with the buyer. The contract to sell the business would contain at least five basic elements that are often ignored when children are involved. Those five contractual elements would typically be:

- Mutual assent of both the buyer and the seller;
- A valid offer and acceptance, in writing;
- Adequate consideration (meaning money or other assets changing hands);

- Both parties having capacity (meaning each has the mental acuity to act on their own behalf);
- All parties have legal standing to negotiate, amend, and execute the contract.

When parents sell or pass the family business to a child, it is likely they only sporadically adhere to these basic contractual elements. Parents will often dictate the terms of the agreement, thus denying mutual assent. It is commonplace for parents to sell or transfer the business to their children for less than its fair market value, often without any money changing hands. Finally, even though the parent and child may have the mental acuity to act on their own behalf, it is not unusual to find one or both of the parties did not have separate legal representation. Familial succession can be complicated, but it need not be!

Back in the first chapter, I shared a story of misguided familial succession. I stated the primary reason passing a business down to the next generation is so frequently unsuccessful is because the second generation lacks *skin in the game*. The succession plan is too often based on an *understanding* between the parties, rather than a *contract*. Mom or Dad may not necessarily be interested in making money from their kids. The parents are looking to be comfortable. Assuming they are financially secure, they frequently do not see the need to burden both the children and the enterprise with indebtedness. As such, it is common for the parents to keep the firm in *ownership limbo* by maintaining ownership while the children operate the firm. Unfortunately, knowing they have Mom and/or Dad looking over their proverbial shoulder can be difficult. Is it any wonder so few of these transitions ever pan out?

For a transition to the next generation to work, there needs to be a valid contract—an arm's-length agreement to sell the firm—from parent to child. Absent a valid agreement to transfer and sell the parents' interest to their child or children, with adequate consideration and separate legal representation on both sides, the likelihood of a successful transition from one familial generation to the next is meager, at best.

Key Questions Every Parent Needs to Ask About Familial Succession

For many parents, it is their dream to see their children continue the legacy they started. While this is a worthy goal, there are some important questions a parent should ask *before* considering how (and to whom) to pass the business.

- Is it wise to divide the business equally between children currently working in the business and those not involved?
- Does it make sense to leave the majority—if not the entirety—of the business to the child or children working in the business even though it may create an unequal inheritance?
- If the children who are not involved in the family business do not receive a share of ownership, does it make sense to leave them assets not related to the value of the business, such as life insurance or other assets in the estate?
- How does your spouse feel about giving business assets to children in the business and different assets to those who are not?
- Is there a problem with children outside the business receiving liquid assets while those working in it receive the business, which is an illiquid asset?
- Would it upset your family dynamic if those working in the business begin receiving ownership ahead of the parent/owner's death, while those not involved in the company must wait until their parents die to receive any portion of their inheritance?

Parents rarely, if ever, deliberately make decisions without their children's best interests in mind or with the intent to upset one child in favor of another. However, parental intentions and their vision for succession may or may not line up with their kids' idea of reality. The problem is there are not many "courses" out there to teach parents and adult children how to communicate their succession plans to one another.

The Mass Mutual survey cited earlier states that the vast majority of parent-owners believe they are accomplishing an act of kindness by splitting all their assets, including the family business, equally among their children. However, the sibling working in the business may feel jilted by such an arrangement. When a parent tends to be dictatorial or arbitrary, this conversation can become even more complicated. While everyone knows they will not live forever, knowing the proper time to

> *"While everyone knows they will not live forever, knowing the proper time to step down from company leadership is another matter entirely."*

step down from company leadership is another matter entirely. Difficulties arise when parent-owners are not prepared to face the fact that they will have no choice but to eventually pass leadership to another generation. Patty Azar, one of the premier business coaches in the United States, once told me, "Far too often owners spend the majority of their time working *in* their business instead of *on* their business." Parent-owners who say, "I'm going to let them figure it out when I die," are copping out and could easily be precipitating a horror show in the end.

Family business transitions do not have to end badly. Contention is optional; in fact, it is a choice. When you fail to engage in active communication before succession is on the table, you are setting your family up for contentious times in the future. Transitioning a business within the family takes time, often years. It takes communication and accountability on all sides. It takes a commitment to setting up both the business and the family with a view toward long-term success far in advance. With transparency, open communication, and a willingness to compromise with fairness, a parent-owner can develop a strategy that, while not necessarily equal, *can* be fair.

A Challenging Family Legacy

Rick's father was a second-generation entrepreneur. During the Depression, his grandfather, Gabriel, started a fruit stand. The fruit stand soon morphed into a hamburger stand and, in due time, a restaurant. In their small town, everyone knew "The Gabe" (as Gabriel was known) and the restaurant bearing his nickname. Patrons came to The Gabe for breakfast, lunch, and dinner. By the 1960s, Gabriel and his wife, Kathryn, had parlayed The Gabe into a small real estate conglomerate. They built a multi-story hotel and a grand shopping center in the middle of town. Even though the restaurant was initially the goose laying the golden eggs, over the years, the income from the properties dwarfed that of the restaurant.

Rick's dad grew up working at The Gabe. Around 1970, when Rick was only 12, Gabriel died. Kathryn became the head of the family business, but Rick's dad ran The Gabe. The economy was not kind to the restaurant. Rick's dad would frequently go to his mother to discuss the restaurant's struggles. He advised his mom to close The Gabe, but Kathryn would have no part of it. The business bore her husband's name. It was his legacy. She decided to subsidize the restaurant by moving money from the real estate account to the restaurant account. The restaurant provided jobs to scores of people who had been with them for years. The Gabe originally provided the capital to build the other buildings. Now, the buildings would subsidize the restaurant ... or so she thought.

Ten years after Gabriel died, Kathryn passed. As per her husband's intention, in her will, she left the restaurant to Rick's dad, Larry, and gave her four daughters and her son equal shares in the real estate company. The arrangement was neither fair nor equal. Kathryn's daughters were married and had never been involved in either The Gabe or the real estate firm. When Kathryn became ill, her daughter's husbands began operating the real estate company. In short order, they became aware of how much money was being funneled from the real estate account to subsidize the restaurant. They were incensed. They were certain Rick's father, their brother-in-law, must have either hoodwinked his mother or moved the money without her knowledge. Rather than discussing it with Kathryn or Rick's dad while Kathryn was alive, they decided to wait and deal with it after her death. At Kathryn's funeral, the husbands took Larry aside and informed him he needed to pay back to the real estate company all the money that was "moved" to the restaurant over the past 10 years.

The resulting bitterness fractured the family. Larry could not pay back the money. He tried to fight the family, but as a minority owner in the real estate company, he was consistently outvoted. After only a few years, he ran out of money at the restaurant, and The Gabe went out of business. The five siblings eventually went their separate ways, and several stopped talking to one another. The real estate was eventually sold. Today, there is virtually no tangible evidence Gabriel or Kathryn ever existed in that town. Poor planning, lack of communication, and good old-fashioned greed destroyed a family legacy. Familial succession did this family no favors.

Overcoming the Family Legacy

In the late 1970s, Rick married his high school sweetheart at the tender age of 19. It was just before Kathryn, his grandmother, died. The marriage was challenging from the start. He and his wife had two children, Ricky and Kathy. The acrimony in the family took its toll on Rick's marriage, and when his children were four and one, he and his wife divorced. A year later, Rick met Sherrie. Rick's wife decided to leave their native Ohio and move, with their children, to Florida. Rick was determined to be in his children's lives, and with little keeping him in Ohio, followed his ex-wife to Fort Lauderdale.

After moving to Florida, Rick entered the insurance business and started working with a successful agent in Fort Lauderdale. Before long, on behalf of his mentor, he was pounding the pavement, knocking on the doors of any business that would give him the time of day. Rick is fond of saying he would quit the business every Friday, change his mind over the weekend, and rehire himself on Monday. Rick was nothing if not tenacious.

Soon after moving to Florida, Rick asked Sherrie to join him. They eventually married and had two children. After numerous years working with his mentor, Rick determined it was time to branch out on his own. Instead of walking into his boss' office and quitting, he went to him and said, "Adam, I need your help." So, with Adam's help, Rick started an independent agency two hours north of Fort Lauderdale in Port St. Lucie, Florida. Over the years, Rick, working side by side with Sherrie, built a significant business.

In August 2001, Ricky, his son from his first marriage, graduated from the University of Florida with an MBA in International Business. He was offered a position and was preparing to move to New York City in October 2001 when, less than a month after his graduation, two hijacked airplanes crashed into the World Trade Center in Manhattan. The events of September 11th, 2001, rocked his world (and the planet) forever. His hiring was put on hold as everyone came to grips with the tragedy now known as 9/11.

Rick asked Ricky to consider coming to work with him. Rick paid Ricky more than he should, but you do things for family you may not do for others. From the beginning, Rick saw Ricky's potential. Even though at times he struggled, Ricky had a keen insight for operations and understood the insurance marketplace. In due time, he became a key player in the company.

Rick and Sherrie also worked closely together. Unfortunately, the friction between her and her stepson was always lurking just under the surface. Even though she adored Ricky, there was always an uneasiness in their relationship. Rick's first wife did not like Sherrie. She consistently went out of her way to influence her children's minds negatively about Rick's second wife. Sherrie was different from both Rick and his first wife. She had been raised in a relatively poor family. Her father was a coal miner, and her parents and siblings never traveled out of their home state. She frequently felt like Rick spoiled Ricky and his daughter, and it became a point of contention between them.

In the early 2000s, the agency began to blossom. They added several additional locations and moved their headquarters a few miles south of Port St. Lucie to Stuart. After graduating with an accounting degree from Rollins College in Winter Park, just north of Orlando, Rick's daughter, Kathy, joined her father's firm as an in-house accountant. The company grew significantly in the first decade of the 21st century, and Ricky and Kathy played a significant role in the growth. On the flip side, Sherrie and Rick's two sons did not have an interest in the insurance agency. Their eldest son, Barry, had significant health issues, and their youngest, Cameron, had his eye set on earning a doctorate and becoming a university professor.

Barry's health was beginning to take up more and more of their time. They often traveled across the country, trying to help their son as he battled his illness. In due time, their son's health appeared to turn a corner, and Rick and Sherrie decided to set him up in a business of his own. Unfortunately, the illness quickly came back, and they were forced to sell their son's company. Inevitably, Barry's health problems were taking them away from work frequently and began to wear them out emotionally. Fortunately, Ricky continued to build the agency by initiating state-of-the-art marketing strategies to expand their reach locally and beyond.

Rick and Sherrie were mentally exhausted. They started to consider selling the business, and Ricky was their first (and ultimately *only*) candidate. Rick and Sherrie had set aside funds for their two children. Barry, with the health challenges, was never married, and because of savvy investments made by his father on his behalf, he was financially secure. Cameron did not make much money as an assistant professor and struggled financially, even with his parents' assistance. Rick and Sherrie had what has become the modern family—two marriages, multiple children from each marriage, and complicated relationships throughout.

Rick and Sherrie had a long conversation with Ricky and his sister, Kathy, who worked in the business, and decided to sell a majority interest to them. They never appraised the company. They came up with a number that was comfortable to Rick and Sherrie, took their plan to their attorney, and drafted the agreement. Ricky and Kathy obtained a small business loan for the down payment and set up a long-term payment plan for the balance. As is the case with many family businesses, they settled on a valuation that was significantly under fair market value[2]. Rick and Sherrie were happy to structure the sale with a nominal down payment and the balance structured as a loan payable over several years. They had no intention to overburden the company with debt, and since the small business loan was only for the down payment, they had little problem securing the bank financing they needed to execute the agreement.

Throughout the entire process of selling the agency, the goal was to avoid creating enmity between the four children. Rick also wanted to make sure Barry and Cameron, his two sons with Sherrie, were taken care of, and purchased life insurance on Sherrie and himself to assure the two boys received something close to the value of the business after he and their mother died. Shortly after the sale of the agency closed, things changed dramatically for the better in the agency. Ricky had a remarkable grasp on the new national health care plan introduced by President Obama, known as the Affordable Care Act or Obamacare. Ricky became an Obamacare expert and expanded the scope of the agency's business in ways no one, except possibly Ricky, saw coming. Every month after Ricky took charge, the company's size, profit share, volume, and profitability exploded. Only three years after the purchase, the company's volume was up tenfold and caught the attention of a national firm looking to buy large agencies specializing in Obamacare. The agency was suddenly being courted by people with extremely deep pockets, and they were being offered nearly 20 times what Rick had received for the company!

Ricky and Kathy decided to merge the agency with the national firm, with the blessing of their father, making the two of them incredibly wealthy. Regrettably, the value they received for the agency created tremendous angst in the family. Cameron, the professor, wanted to know why he was not given the opportunity to purchase shares from his dad, even though he had never been involved and lacked the financial capacity to purchase shares. And, although his health problems left him 100% disabled, their eldest son, Barry, felt similarly. Sherrie believed Rick was, once again, far too generous with Ricky and Kathy when they sold the business. The very acrimony he was trying to avoid became a reality.

Perception Becomes Reality

Familial succession is not easy. It is never without its challenges because it is about family. Rick's story—which is true, except for the names and places involved—points out several of the many challenges inherent in familial succession. It is never fair. It is never equal. It is rarely arm's-length. Family members tend to be emotional, especially when money is involved.

Is it any wonder that nearly all the proverbial seven deadly sins—pride, lying, wrath, scheming, backbiting, envy, and my favorite, instigating unnecessary conflict[3]—are frequently found in familial succession plans? With all the challenges involved in familial successions, one could argue it is miraculous any businesses succeed in passing from one generation to the next!

A lawyer who specializes in family succession once told me, "Inevitably, [when it comes to familial succession] someone in the family **perceives** they have been slighted, even when in **reality** they have not been slighted at all. Too frequently, one or more siblings think the other sibling was handed the crown jewels while they were left to share in the leftovers. Typically, nothing could be farther from the truth …

"Familial succession is not easy."

but good luck convincing the sibling who thinks they were wronged!"

The Prodigal Son

There is a parable Jesus tells known as the parable of the prodigal son[4]. In the story, a father has two sons. The younger son, whom Jesus calls the prodigal, asks his father for his inheritance long before it is appropriate[5]. No one should ever ask a parent for an inheritance while their parent is still alive! Remarkably, the father grants his son's request. The prodigal takes his inheritance (as the song goes) and wastes it on wine, women, and song. After selling his father's goods, he wastes the proceeds and ends up penniless.

What I find most interesting about this story is when the prodigal son acted as though his father was dead, he violated every standard of decency. The irony is the father was not dead, but the son might as well have been. In the end, the supposed dead father gives his *dead son* a chance to live again.

In desperation, the prodigal decides to return home and appeal to his father's mercy. Empty-handed and without an intent to subvert his family, he begs his father to allow him back as a servant. To the son's surprise, the prodigal is not scorned by his father. In fact, the father throws a party for his lost son and welcomes him back with open arms. His brother is furious!

How could his father welcome back his reckless brother? In exasperation, he refuses to have any part in the festivities. He says to his father, "Look! For so many years, I have been serving you and have never neglected a command of yours, and yet you have never given me a [goat], that I might [celebrate] with my friends. But when this son of yours came, who has devoured your wealth with harlots, you killed the fattened calf for him!"

"[The father] said to [the son], 'My child, you have always been with me, and all that is mine is yours. But we had to [celebrate] and rejoice, for this brother of yours was dead and has begun to live; was lost and has been found.'"[6]

Family Is Messy

The bottom line? Family is messy! The truth is, most families are made up of common, ordinary, broken, screwed-up, and often scandalous people. We more often live in a condition of not-togetherness rather than togetherness. I presume every family is messy. There are inconsistent messy families. There are up and down messy families; in and out messy families; now I trust you, now I don't, messy families; now I love you, now I don't messy families. The messy list is a mess.

> *"The bottom line? Family is messy!"*

There is no secret sauce in overcoming messiness in a family. There is no secret formula to becoming a functional family. There is no test you can take to prove you know how to do family well. You can be the most competent person in the world and be completely incompetent when it comes to family. Most of all, family is not about perfection; it is about acceptance. Family is a complex, complicated, convoluted, perplexing, disorderly, sloppy, chaotic look at preordained relationships in an imperfect world. Even more, familial relationships do not chart in a straight line. Our family relationships are mixed-up, topsy-turvy, helter-skelter toboggan rides full of unexpected turns, bruising bumps, and bone-breaking collisions. Nevertheless, here is the truth about family—although your family may be crazy, flawed, and messy, it is still worth protecting.

There are no perfect families, so embrace the messiness! Expect your brother to be a prodigal and mess up. Do not be surprised by something Mom or Dad says. Too many families show up looking outwardly contented and at peace with one another, but inwardly they are crying out for someone to intervene and heal the brokenness. Love your family just as they are—confused, complicated, frustrated, often frightened, guilty, and unable to communicate among themselves. Have the courage to admit your family has struggles, but you must *choose* to never give up on family.

CHAPTER 10

ARE YOU READY?

S everal years ago, my wife, Grace, and I traveled to Scotland. As an avid golfer, I brought my clubs with the specific intention of playing as much golf as my bride would allow. Upon exiting our plane, we headed straight to St. Andrews Golf Links, the home of arguably the most famous golf course in the world, *The Old Course*. Having played golf since age 12, this was a lifelong dream come true.

First thing the next morning, I went on the balcony of our hotel room overlooking the Old Course. As I gazed out over the 17th fairway, it was surreal. The sun rising over the North Sea, along with the dream-like mist coming off the carpeted foreground, reminded me of what Michael Murray penned in my favorite golf book of all time, *Golf in the Kingdom*:

> "Oh, golf is for smellin' heather & cut grass & walkin' fast across
> the countryside & feelin' the wind
> & watchin' the sun go down & seein' yer friends hit good
> shots & hittin' some yerself.
> It's love & it's feelin' the splendor o' this good world."[1]

There is no essay entitled Football, Basketball, Soccer, or Baseball in the Kingdom. Only golf allows every person—young, old, male, female, regardless of ability, race, color, or creed—to experience the same game, on the same venue, as those who combat at the highest level! I was about to walk the hallowed grounds and feel the splendor o' this good world.

Even in July, the chill in Scotland's morning air is invigorating. As I made my way out the southside of the hotel, I peered out over the tightly cropped fairway until my eyes trained on the 17th green of the Old Course. Subconsciously, I envisioned the Japanese champion, Tommy Nakajima, stroking this beautiful putt from the front of the green in the 1978 Open, toward a hole tucked cagily in the back left. Ruthlessly, the ball catches the subtle ridge, obvious now in the morning light, and trickles into the bunker. Four mighty blasts later, he extricates the ball, but the tournament is lost!

My eyes then made their way up the 18th over the Swilcan Bridge and the Burn splitting the 1st and 18th fairways, and my mind's eye now subconsciously sees Doug Sanders, decked out in pink from head to toe like a flamingo, settling over a three-foot putt to win *The Open* in 1970, only to push it slightly off its intended path. The next day, Jack Nicklaus would best him in a playoff and forever make Doug Sanders a footnote in golfing lore.

What an incredible thing the mind is. Instead of seeing Seve Ballesteros shaking his fist and jumping up and down when he won in 1984, I saw Sanders losing. Instead of envisioning Jack Nicklaus, or Tiger Woods, or Zach Johnson, or Long John Daly, all winners at St. Andrews in *The Open*, my mind mustered two of the greatest calamities in the history of the sport from deep within its childhood memory bank. I pondered absently, "Was this a harbinger of what was yet to come?"

NATO Golf

When I arrived at the first tee of the Old Course at the appointed time, some 12 hours after I rose, my excitement had only grown. My assigned caddie was a strapping young Kiwi in his late 20s named James. Only the week before, James had competed in the British Amateur on these very links. I vividly remember him coming over to me, and after the pleasantries asking, "Well, how do you play, mate?" Which is code for, "Are you any good?"

"I play to an 8 [handicap]," I replied, which means half the time I am good, and half the time, I stink.

"OK, are you ready?"

"Oh, yeah, I have been dreaming about breaking 80 on the Old Course since I booked the trip."

"Hmm."

With that, I hit a perfect drive just short of the Swilcan Burn, pitched it on the green, only to three-putt for bogie. On the second, it went left, then right, then left again—double bogie. On the third, the military golf—left, right, left, right—continued. After holing out for my third double bogie on the par-5 fifth, I stood 8 over par, and my dream of shooting 80 now required me to be even par the remaining 13 holes.

Up to now, James had not said much. As we walked off the fifth green, he saw my befuddled look and said, "Are you ready to play golf now?"

"What have we been doing for the last five holes?"

"Mate, you may have thought you were ready, but it is clear you were not. How about we play NATO Golf?"

"NATO Golf?" I asked.

"It is what I call *not attached to outcome* golf. Let's learn NATO Golf."

"I don't get it," I said.

"Mate, you are obsessed with a score. Forget about your score. When adversity came, you were not ready. You were not ready mentally, emotionally, or strategically, so you messed up. There are lots of ways to hit bad shots and one way to hit good ones—with your genuine swing. When you are ready mentally, emotionally, and strategically, your genuine swing will just pour out of you. When you are concerned about outcome, the opposite happens. You lose your genuine swing."

> *"Golf, like most everything in life, is played one shot at a time."*

He was right. When you are not ready, golf is ridiculously hard. Golf, like most everything in life, is played one shot at a time. After every shot on the first five holes, I was thinking about the shot I *already* hit and the disaster sure to come.

Finding Your Genuine Swing

When we arrived at the sixth tee, he said, "See your genuine swing and then *swing that swing*." I decided not to approach it, the ball, that is, until I saw *my* genuine swing hitting the ball. Almost mystically, the clutter cleared, I pulled back the club and hit the most solid shot I had hit all day.

As we approached the ball, my heart began to sink. Instead of a perfect result, the ball was sitting in the middle of what I can call a "bird's nest" of twigs and grass. As amazing as the shot felt on the tee, the result was equally impressive ... on the other side of the spectrum!

"NATO!" James said. I smiled. Instead of whining about the misfortune, I pitched the ball out into the fairway, hit the next shot close to the hole, and made the putt. My first par at St. Andrews!

"NATO!"

I made par on the next hole, and on the par-3 eighth, my shot landed 4 inches from the hole, and I made my first birdie!

"NATO!"

We started chatting, and the score became less and less important. Before long, we arrived at the 14th hole—a 530-yard par-5 and home to the infamous *Hell Bunker,* located about 100 yards short of the 14th green, which must be avoided at all cost. My mind began thinking about what I had to avoid—*future* mistakes—rather than making my genuine swing on the shot at hand. I vividly remember thinking mid-swing, "Do not make the big mistake and hit this right!" Of course, the ball went flying out toward the left, hit the right turn signal, and was last seen heading west toward Glasgow! Without missing a beat, James whispers in my ear, "No worries, mate! Nicklaus once did the same thing. Genuine swing—NATO."

Perfectly Imperfect

The obvious question here is, "What has this story got to do with succession planning?" *More than you might imagine.* Being outcome-driven is great when everything works out according to plan. The problem is life rarely goes according to plan. It is usually more like my golf game. The outcome rarely matches the expectation, and disappointment is bound to follow.

This is especially true when it comes to choosing a successor. The plan is to find the "perfect person," but the perfect person does not exist. The real goal is to discover the perfect *imperfect* person, who is the *right* fit.

Even though decades have passed, everything about my day at St. Andrews endures. Attachment to outcome is a sure-fire way to end up disappointed, which, in my experience, reveals itself in anger, anxiety, frustration, and/or indecision.

I have met far too many Type-A personalities walking around with a submerged, low-grade anger, who are an incident away from combustion caused by the way things have gone in their life. Anger, used to mask anxiety, frequently leads to decision-phobia, the fear of making another mistake. Mahatma Gandhi famously said, "Freedom is not worth having if it does not include the freedom to make mistakes."[2] In an attempt to avoid mistakes, it is easy to stop taking risks. Succession is a risk worth taking, even though there is no assurance of the outcome.

> *"Not being attached to outcome is one of the greatest secrets most people never learn."*

Not being attached to outcome is one of the greatest secrets most people never learn. It is key to being mentally, emotionally, strategically, and financially ready to sell a business and let someone else take your place.

A Lesson In Succession from the Miami Heat

Ever since their first game in the old Miami Arena against the Sacramento Kings in 1988, I have been a Miami Heat fan. Erik Spoelstra and Pat Riley joined the Heat together in 1995. Pat came to the Heat with hundreds of wins under his belt, four NBA Championships, and three NBA Coach of the Year titles. Erik started as the video coordinator, *whatever that is.*

When Heat owner Mickey Arison hired Riley, he had a plan. He asked Riley to be head coach and president of basketball operations. His intent was to have Pat develop a coaching successor and then take over the front office operations of the team.

I never thought Pat Riley would step down as head coach. I thought he would coach until he died, but I was wrong. Pat was committed to finding the right successor. He thought it would be long-time assistant Stan Van Gundy. In 2003, Riley stepped down and elevated Van Gundy from assistant coach to head coach. Even though Stan was a good choice, Riley was not ready to step away from coaching. He stepped away before he was ready to stop. After two seasons, Van Gundy resigned, Riley returned, and Riley led Miami to their first NBA Championship in 2006.

After the next season, Riley resigned as coach and shocked the world when he elevated former video coordinator Erik Spoelstra, an unknown assistant, to head coach. Erik was hand-picked by Pat Riley and has since become one of the longest-tenured head coaches in the NBA. There are some great lessons you can learn about being ready to exit from how Riley stepped away from coaching.

Mentally Prepared

When Riley elevated Spoelstra, unlike with Van Gundy, Reilly was mentally ready to toss the keys to Spoelstra and Erik was prepared to lead. Even though people say they have business plans, in my experience, many spend more time planning their vacations and Christmas parties than they do their continuity plans.

Other than starting the company, transitioning to another leader is the most important financial event in an owner's life. For many, the value of their business is the largest single asset they possess. Making sure they have thought through their exit and given it the attention it deserves is not optional.

Like Riley, for a founder to be ready to exit, they need to be confident they have an Erik Spoelstra and can see themselves in an alternate role. I know a former financial advisor in New England who loves photography. Since he sold his practice, he has traveled the world using his artistic gift. When he was running his business, he did not have the time to do what he is doing today. The practice is thriving under the new leadership. Once a client called him and said, "John, thank you for finding Michael for us." This is precisely what every mentor wants to hear about their chosen aspirant.

These questions can help you determine if you are mentally prepared for succession:

- What would my life look like if someone else was leading the business?
- What other things have I *meant* to do but have not had the time to pull off?
- Assuming money is not an issue, what other things would I consider doing?
- Is my identity tied to my business?

When a person can see someone else leading the firm and see themselves in another role, they are closer to being mentally ready to toss the keys to the next generation of leadership than they realize.

Emotional Readiness

Beyond being mentally prepared, do not underestimate the importance of being emotionally ready to exit. One of the hardest things for high achievers to do is to detach themselves emotionally from their business. The business is their *baby*, after all. They birthed it. They nurtured it. It is emotionally hard to let it go! However, one of the best things my beloved business coach, Patty Azar, said was, "A business is a means to an end, not an end unto itself." She was quick to advise me to look at the company as I would any investment in a portfolio. She described this as approaching the business with an investor's mindset.

Becoming emotionally detached from your *baby* is challenging, but not impossible. What is extremely difficult for most successful high achievers is to consider exiting when the business is on top. Even if it really is what is best for everyone else long-term, until a high-achieving business owner is ready to exit, they are not going anywhere—nor should they.

I learned a great lesson about being emotionally unattached to a business when I was with E.F. Hutton & Company. I participated in the employee stock purchase plan and 401(k) from the time I was eligible. When Hutton was forced out of business, the stock I had been buying for $40-$60/share weeks before was suddenly less than $10/share. Although I had a small amount of stock, I learned a big lesson. I not only lost my job; I lost a significant part of my savings, as well.

The oldest adage in investing is to *buy low and sell high*. I contend this is advice people give lip service, but rarely utilize. No one wants to sell a stock when it just hit a record high, yet that is exactly what the adage suggests! When you begin to look at your business through the lens of an investor, you realize, strictly from a financial perspective, the best time to sell an investment is when its value is up, not down.

Taking the emotion out of selling is a hinge pin to successful exits. This is only possible when the company is evaluated from the viewpoint of an investor. In the eighth chapter, I wrote, "You must not make decisions based on fear." Decisions made in fear often lead to regret, as Jerry experienced when he sold his business to Charles. No one wants to get to the end of their career, wondering, "What if?" Regret is a powerful emotion. Regret clouds thinking and can destroy an exit plan either early or, in Jerry's case, late. Ignore it at your peril.

A large part of emotional readiness is for a leader to be able to see themselves in an alternate role. This is a big challenge among many professionals. It is mind-boggling how many people have told me they feel like they would go stir-crazy if they sold their practice.

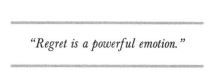

"Regret is a powerful emotion."

"If I am no longer treating patients," one doctor, who was in his 70s, told me, "then who am I?" It is common to attach your identity to your profession. On the other side, one person after another, including myself, who prepared themselves to exit, are loving the next chapter of their life.

The earlier you start thinking about an eventual exit, the easier it becomes to be emotionally prepared to do so, even if it is 25 years from now. I started thinking about succession in the late 1990s when our company was in its infancy. I was less than 40 years old and years away from an eventual exit. I began thinking, preparing, and, most of all, talking about what transitioning the company to someone else might look like, decades ago. As a result, I relished the idea of selling the company and doing other things. It was never something, like my doctor friend, I dreaded. No matter where a person is in the business cycle, they should be exploring mentally what their exit might look like.

Strategic Readiness

As said previously, making sure a firm is strategically ready for a founder's exit is vital to the ongoing success of the company after the leadership changes. Implementing the right processes and installing the right people are essential. While the price a seller receives is important, when the firm is strategically ready for a transition, it has a greater chance of not only surviving, but *thriving* after the owner exits. Certainly, no one wants the departure of the founder to negatively impact the firm, but it can, and often does, when the founder leaves and the business was not strategically prepared to continue without its founder.

I wrote previously about the importance of finding the right successor, but how important is the implementation of the right processes?

Miami Heat head coach Erik Spoelstra uses the word *process* constantly. The editor of Slice Miami, Josh Baumgard, is fond of saying Spoelstra invented "the process." Probably not, but Erik believes completely in focusing on process and letting the results take care of themselves. To Spoelstra, the process is more than a strategic plan. It also includes staying the course, embracing adversity, not getting ahead of yourself, and not dwelling on the past. One night, after a particularly tough loss, I remember vividly Erik saying, "The [NBA] Championship is not won or lost until the final game in June. We trust the process."

The process, in Erik Spoelstra's world, is about giving his team the best opportunity to win. The process starts by putting strategic ways of operating in place to allow everyone on the team the opportunity to excel. In sport, if players are out of shape, the chance of winning drops wantonly. However, when they are out of sorts mentally, the chance of succeeding drops exponentially. For example, in the 2016-17 season, the Miami Heat lost 30 of their first 41 games halfway through the season. To say their record was dismal is an understatement. They were dead last in their conference.

Spoelstra was disappointed. His players were upset. The fans were disillusioned. Nevertheless, Spoelstra stuck with *the process*, and in the second half of the season, the team turned their record upside down, winning the exact number of games in the final 41 games (30), they had lost in the first half of the season with essentially the same roster. Although they missed the playoffs, the turnaround was unprecedented. Nine games into the second half of the season—all wins, by the way—a reporter asked, "Erik, you have been right in the middle of the win streak and the turnaround, but for someone on the outside, how would you explain an 11-30 team winning 9 in a row?"

His answer says it all. "It has not been about the result for us," he said. "If you have been around the team, you have seen the progress. I mentioned it through the losses that we felt our team was getting better. Throughout all of it, you must maintain perspective. Day after day, you need to focus on each day as it comes to improve." He finished by saying, "You are never as good as you think you are, and you are never as bad as you think you are."

> *"You are never as good as you think you are, and you are never as bad as you think you are."*

Let's look at six specific processes that can be implemented now to prepare the founder, successor, and business to be strategically prepared when a founder exits.

1. Promote Effective Strategies

The correct process and most effective strategies always put the team in the best position to win. A strategically prepared business has a process of effective strategies it uses to grow the business and build exceptional results. When a firm is growing, it is going to make mistakes. Learning from those mistakes is just as important as the strategies the firm promotes. Do not fear mistakes—just make sure no one ignores them. High achievers like to think they are always performing at peak effectiveness. The problem is, as Erik said, you are never as good, or as bad, as you think you are. The goal needs to be to perform at peak effectiveness, one client and one transaction at a time. As my caddie, James, put it, let everyone find their *genuine swing*—the one that, in the crucible of competition, works best for them! Most of all, do not write your championship speech when you still have a three-foot putt to make or a free throw to shoot! As Yogi Berra famously said, "It ain't over 'til it's over."

2. Promote Tangible Skills and Habits

Make sure the successor and staff have the tangible skills, coupled with good habits, to give the firm the greatest chance to succeed. Skills are often wasted when not combined with exceptional habits. However, there is a myth that says people struggle because of a lack of discipline—this is simply not true! There is no more disciplined species than human beings.

We are all fully disciplined to a certain set of habits. Successful people have ingrained effective habits into their process, while unsuccessful people have ingrained ineffective habits into their routine. A lack of discipline is the exception, not the rule. So, adopt better habits!

> *"We are all fully disciplined to a certain set of habits."*

3. Promote Reading

Never underestimate the importance of purposeful reading. Reading books, magazines, and articles is essential to growth. Books are to humans as water and fertilizer are to plants. The kind of things people read is more important than the volume of the reading. Since the invention of the Guttenberg Press, the availability of reading material has exploded. With the introduction and acceptance of electronic mediums, we are now inundated with information to absorb. Yet, research conducted by the Pew Research Center and the National Endowment of the Arts indicates many people are spending inordinate amounts of time reading material that will never improve their lives. Think social media, for example.

167

Warren Buffett was once asked what his best habit was. According to a 2019 article in INC magazine, he said, "Read 500 pages like this every day. That's how knowledge works. It builds up, like compound interest. All of you can do it, but I guarantee not many of you will do it."[3]

While I cannot say for certain Warren Buffett reads 500 pages a day, I can confirm reading consumes much of the time of ultra-successful people. The list of prolific readers is a who's who of the ultra-successful. Elon Musk, Bill Gates, Mark Zuckerberg, Oprah Winfrey, Cheryl Sandberg, Mark Cuban, are just a few of on an endless list of incessant readers! These are not the exceptions; they are the rule.

Steve Siebold, author of *How Rich People Think*, has interviewed over 1,200 multimillionaires. He wrote, "Walk into a wealthy person's home and one of the first things you'll see is an extensive library of books they've used to educate themselves on how to become more successful," Siebold wrote. "The middle class, if they read at all, reads novels, tabloids, and entertainment magazines."[4] According to Siebold, even modestly wealthy people read primarily for self-improvement and success, while poorer people spend most of their time on social media and entertainment sites.

4. Promote Productivity

One of the greatest wastes of time is email. The average person is inundated hourly, even on weekends, with productivity-sapping emails. This inefficiency needs to stop! Do not permit emails to dictate your schedule. Far too many people spend too much time on emails, voicemails, and texts. However, the way you choose to deal with these time wasters is habitual. Make the decision now to deal with them on *your* terms, not on the *sender's* terms.

First, be careful to whom you give an email address. Avoid subscribing and unsubscribe from what is unimportant. Second, respond to email, voicemail, and texts at a scheduled time, not more than twice a day. Emails, texts, voicemails, Facebook, Twitter, Instagram, and all other social media sites keep you busy, but squelch productivity.

A friend, who is a surgeon, has mastered the art of maximized productivity. She realized, almost from the start of her career, she was helping the most people and making the most money for her practice when she was performing surgery. As such, she spends as much time as humanly possible in surgery and reading, and delegates nearly everything else. She says, "Every hour I am in surgery makes our practice thousands of dollars. I only have a certain number of hours I am prepared to work. Why would I spend time doing $20/hour tasks, when I could be doing $2,000/hour tasks?"

5. Promote Excellence

Closely related to developing good habits is promoting excellence. Companies are only as strong as what they expect from every member of the firm. Strategically prepared firms expect employee excellence. Nevertheless, excellence rises and falls on leadership, and it is up to leaders to set the standard.

Every person working at a company, from the CEO to the front desk clerk, needs to be punctual, putting clients first, finishing tasks on a timely and proficient basis, and demanding exceptional performance out of themselves and their colleagues. No one should be afraid to call a colleague out who is not living up to a standard of excellence. It should be the minimum requirement, the least everyone should expect. Excellence is not a suggestion. It is a prerequisite, exampled first by those in leadership, and at the heart of the firm's culture.

"If mediocrity is tolerated, it is not a personnel failure but a failure of leadership."

If mediocrity is tolerated, it is not a personnel failure but a failure of leadership.

6. Move Forward—Fail Forward

Finally, always move forward. If you watch great athletes hit a ball, the one constant is the best players drive forward as they hit the ball and always finish on their front foot. The weight of a baseball player is always transferred to the front leg after the ball is thrown or hit. Look at tennis players, soccer players, golfers, football players, volleyball players, boxers, runners, skaters—you name it. When they fall back, their performance suffers.

Closely tied to moving forward is failing forward. John Maxwell, in his book entitled, *Failing Forward*, wrote, "The difference between average people and [high] achieving people is their perception of and response to failure. Most people are never prepared to deal with failure." Maxwell says, if you are like him, coming out of school, you "feared [failure], misunderstood [failure], and ran away from [failure]." In Maxwell's words, "Make failure a friend, not a nemesis."[5]

Suffice it to say, everyone fails. Look at Jonas Salk, the inventor of the polio vaccine. He is said to have developed over 200 failed polio vaccines before he developed an effective one. He said he had not failed, he merely discovered 200 ways *not* to vaccinate for polio before he finally found a way *to* vaccinate for it. Thomas Edison, the Wright brothers, Alexander Graham Bell, Leonardo da Vinci, and Isaac Newton failed innumerable times before they succeeded. The difference was they allowed their failure to push them forward, not set them back.

Effective failure prepared them for success.

Financial Readiness

To be ready to execute a succession plan, the founder and business must not only be ready mentally, emotionally, and strategically, both the founder and the business need to be financially prepared when the founder exits.

Let me tell it to you straight: Being financially prepared to exit is never an option—it is essential. For many years, my wife and I have been committed to living on much less than we could. I came up with the expression "Living on 80" many years ago as part of a teaching series Steve Scalici and I created called *Five Years to Freedom*. The idea is to create a budget where you purposely learn to live on 80% (or less) of what you earn. When you live on 80, by definition, you stay out of debt. The 20% margin gives you a buffer if, for some reason, your income drops. Furthermore, the arrangement allows you to invest money on a regular, ongoing basis for the long term because the key element is to pay yourself first. In other words, you carve the 20% off the top of your earnings rather than trying to carve it out of what is left over.

Spoiler alert: There is never anything left over in business! There are five words that determine everything in your financial life: *spend less than you can.*

> *"Spoiler alert: There is never anything left over in business!"*

Over the years, I have seen too many people, many of whom I would call colleagues, become financial wrecks through overindulgence and poor money management. Frankly, in my early days after moving to Stuart, I found myself getting carried away with a new, more abundant lifestyle. Even though I was earning more money than I had ever contemplated, I allowed my lifestyle to consume the income almost as fast as I could earn it.

When you are doing well, you can get away with poor money management for a while, but once we started our company, I knew it would take several years before the income would be back to what it was in my previous role. After several years of not paying as much attention to my consumptive lifestyle, starting a new company from scratch changed everything. I needed to pay greater attention to all things financial to ensure we did not go broke as we developed the company. I needed a guide to escort us because spending without thinking was not on the ballot.

A dear colleague (who has since died) collared me one Sunday afternoon and gave me what was then a brand-new book entitled *The Four Laws of Debt Free Prosperity*.[6] This book is, without a doubt, the most important book, other than the Bible, I have ever read. It transformed my views on spending and saving money. I have since given this book to hundreds of people, and I have personally been living by its principles for over 25 years. The book outlines four laws, and I added a fifth. These five "laws" are as simple as they are difficult:

1. **Track Everything**: Pay strict attention to where you spend money, whether by cash, check, or credit cards.
2. **Target Spending and Saving**: Proactively decide where you spend and save money.
3. **Trim Waste**: Eliminate unproductive or unnecessary spending.
4. **Train**: Become financially literate.
5. **Treat and Give**: Be prepared to do something nice for yourself and give to others.

These five rules have proven invaluable in allowing me to have the financial readiness to exit my business without the fear of inadequate financial resources. When you keep track of where money goes, you do not waste money, and it is easier to create targets as to where the money should go. Every financial advisor knows if a metric cannot be measured, it cannot be managed. Setting financial goals and living within your means is not restrictive. On the contrary, it gives you a massive amount of financial freedom. Best of all, the more you pay attention to your finances, the more financially literate you will become, the better you will be able to serve your clients, the more fun you will have with the spending you do enjoy, and the more you will be able to give to charity and to those less fortunate.

Are You Ready To Exit?

I entitled this chapter *Are You Ready* because unless you are prepared to exit, the likelihood of leaving seamlessly is uncertain. Do not allow discouragement and outcome attachment to keep you from continuing to look for the right successor. Remember the NATO acronym: *Not Attached to Outcome.* Stay committed to finding the right person without worrying about the result. Do not be afraid to make mistakes; just do not ignore them.

Get mentally prepared to toss the keys to a successor as early as possible. Secondly, take the emotion out of the decision to exit. I call this being emotionally ready. Look at the business in the same way an investor would view it. Be prepared to sell when things are at their best, not heading downward. Third, before you move forward, make sure the business is strategically prepared as well. Go back and re-read the section on strategic readiness, and make sure the company is prepared for the founder to leave. Finally, make sure your personal financial house is in order *before* you sell the business. Even though the value of the business most likely represents much of your net worth, make sure your personal financial condition is strong enough to allow you to leave with or without the proceeds of the sale of the business.

So, I will ask you again: *Are you ready?*

CHAPTER 11

THE 10 COMMANDMENTS

I nevitably, when I speak with someone considering selling their business, they are bound to ask:

"How much is my company worth?" The answer is, *it depends*—on the business, and you.

Imagine two scenarios. In the first scenario, a person comes waltzing into your office looking to buy your business. You think to yourself, what is the most outrageous amount that I would ask this person to pay for the company? Once you have that number in your head, imagine a second scenario where the government has decided to tax the value of every company in the country. What is the amount you would want the government to appraise the business for tax purposes? Somewhere between those two numbers is what your company is worth. When it comes to a sales price, this adage certainly applies: A business is worth precisely what someone is willing to pay for it—nothing more and nothing less.

> *"A business is worth precisely what someone is willing to pay for it— nothing more and nothing less."*

In this chapter, I will outline what I call the 10 Commandments of buying and selling a small business. While these commandments are not as absolute as the 10 Commandments given to Moses, to maximize the value of the firm and complete the transaction properly, they should not be ignored. With that in mind, like the 10 Commandments given to Moses, the first three commandments, if ignored or disobeyed, are done so at one's peril:

1. Thou shalt not, **under any circumstances**, *do it yourself.*
2. Thou shalt not, **under any circumstances**, *share counsel.* Get your own lawyer, and do not sign an agreement unvetted by your own counsel!
3. Thou shalt not, **under any circumstances**, *sell without an Agreement,* even if it is with family.

This is one of the largest transactions most people ever make. Do it right.[1]

Now, let's look at these Commandments.

Commandment #1:
Thou Shalt Not Do It Yourself

This axiom is sure: *He who represents himself has a fool for a client.* It is a bad idea for anyone to represent themselves, *even if* the buyer or seller is a lawyer, a tax professional, a mergers and acquisitions expert, a financial advisor, or someone else who works in this arena.

Buyers and sellers hurt themselves, sometimes irreparably, when they fail to engage legal counsel who can provide unbiased advice. In fact, not hiring *competent* professionals may cost more in the long run than doing it yourself might appear to be saving in the short term.

The key word in the last sentence is competent. The Oxford English Dictionary defines *competence* as "having the necessary ability, knowledge, or skill to do something successfully."[2] Engage

> *"Incompetent counsel is as bad, if not worse, than doing it yourself."*

advisors with the necessary ability, knowledge, and skill to do the transaction successfully. Incompetent counsel is as bad, if not worse, than doing it yourself.

The goals of the buyer and seller are not mutually exclusive. Sellers want to maximize the net proceeds from the sale and be assured they have found the right person to serve their clients and lead their employees. Buyers want to maximize value and obtain additional clientele and employees while reducing the risk inherent in the transaction. Competent advice improves the odds of satisfying both the needs of the seller and the buyer exponentially. Done properly, the result is a win-win-win—a win for the seller, a win for the buyer, and a win for the clients. To paraphrase Steven Covey, from his famous book *The Seven Habits of Highly Effective People*, if it is not win-win, call the whole thing off!

Engaging professionals helps balance the scales and keeps you in compliance with the first and most important commandment of buying and selling—*thou shalt not do it yourself.* This is not a DIY project.

Commandment #2:
Thou Shalt Not Share Counsel

There may be nothing worse than attempting to do this yourself, but thinking you can share the same counsel is just as bad an idea. This commandment is often violated when the parties are family members. That said, attorneys cannot represent both parties to an agreement, even if the parties are related. If you think an attorney can represent both a father and his son in the same transaction, you are mistaken. The attorney works for one side or the other, not both. When you attempt to share counsel, usually in an attempt to save money, you are actually violating the first commandment because the one who did not hire the attorney, is, in fact, representing themselves.

While using a single appraisal company may be acceptable, each party should hire separate CPA and merger and acquisition professionals. Be confident your team is prepared to work together to guide you through the myriad of financial considerations involved in the transaction. There is no room for egos and strong personalities derailing the process.

No one would imagine a public company going through a merger or acquisition without separate representation. With what is at stake in the sale of every company, hiring experts is akin to buying insurance. Small to mid-sized companies in the $1-100 million range live below the radar of investment banks and hedge funds. Notwithstanding, some of the best acquisitions are companies of this size. Remember, most people go through this experience just once in their lifetime. Past MDRT President Brian Heckert, a financial advisor in Illinois, has built a small empire by purchasing small books of retirement plan clients throughout middle America. Brian's firm has bought about a dozen books of clients. However, for the people selling, it was their first and probably last business sale. Brian is a great guy. I trust him completely, but who has the advantage in those transactions—the sellers or Brian?

"Hire your own counsel, regardless of who the other party to the transaction happens to be."

The second commandment— *thou shalt not share counsel*—is as important as the first. Hire your own counsel, regardless of who the other party to the transaction happens to be.

Commandment #3:
Thou Shalt Not Purchase Without
a Written Agreement

Handshakes are fine, but they are meaningless when it comes to selling a business. The primary task of the attorney drafting the agreement is to include all the terms the parties have negotiated. While a well-drafted Purchase Agreement not only spells out all the monetary considerations and contingencies of the purchase, it outlines all the non-monetary terms as well. One key non-monetary item is the length of time the seller will continue advising the buyer and/or working with clients after the sale closes.

There are numerous benefits to the owner remaining with the firm post-sale. As I said, retaining existing clientele is important to buyers. When the seller sticks around for a time, it normally results in a smoother transition, better client retention, and gives the buyer the benefit of learning from the seller's experience. This enhances the likelihood of a positive transition once the seller steps away permanently.

While every provision in a Purchase Agreement is important, let's look at three items: the seller's agreement not to compete, taxation, and some of what might be in the fine print that both the buyer and seller should fully understand before signing on the dotted line.

Non-Compete Agreement

In most cases, the seller will be asked to refrain from competing with the business and/or soliciting clients of the firm in any way. In most jurisdictions in the U.S., and in many developed countries around the world, non-compete agreements (sometimes referred to as restrictive covenants) are contractual pacts between the seller and the buyer wherein the seller promises not to compete with the buyer either during the seller's continued employment and/or for a specified time afterward as determined in the agreement.

Every jurisdiction has individual laws dealing with the enforceability of a non-compete agreement. The state of Florida, for example, has a very pro-employer, pro-buyer non-compete statute, with relatively simple precepts. In Florida, a non-compete agreement is enforceable as long as it is for a reasonable length of time (it cannot be permanent), the geographic area is clearly defined (it cannot be everywhere), and it is protecting a legitimate business interest as defined by Florida statutes. While the statutes may not be as straightforward or enforceable in other jurisdictions as they are in Florida, a competent attorney can draft the agreement with language consistent with the laws in your country or state. However, as I said in the first commandment, do not attempt to do this on your own.

Taxation of the Amounts Received Under the Agreement

Often, a portion of the seller's proceeds may be considered compensation and the balance treated as a *capital gain* on either assets or stock in the business. In the United States, the portion allocated as compensation is taxed to the seller as ordinary income subject to ordinary federal and state income tax, as well as Social Security taxes. To the extent the remaining payment represents a gain to the seller, such gain is subject to capital gains tax. In the United States, compensation is a business expense and deductible to the buyer. The amount attributable to the purchase of either assets or stock is not an expense and is not deductible to the buyer. This portion of the proceeds becomes the buyer's tax basis in the assets, or the stock purchased. Once again, it is imperative the seller and the buyer retain legal and tax professionals who understand the tax implications of the sale in their jurisdiction. Taxation can significantly change the net proceeds to the seller and the net cost to the buyer. Make sure the tax implications to both parties are clearly understood BEFORE signing on the dotted line.

The Fine Print

Purchase agreements can be exceptionally long. They can be complex, as they attempt to cover every contingency. While this is not remotely close to a complete list, the agreement will attempt to answer questions like:

- What assets are included and excluded in the sale?
- What liabilities are being assumed by the buyer?
- How is the payout to the seller structured?
- How is the purchase price allocated between compensation and capital?
- Are payments subject to an earn-out provision? If so, how is it structured?
- What are the duties and ongoing responsibilities of each party to the agreement?
- For what period is the seller obligated to continue working with the buyer?
- What are the covenants, representations, and warranties of each party?
- How are defaults and disputes resolved?
- Where and when does the sale close?

Pay attention to the non-compete agreement, taxation, and the fine print. As a rule, if either party does not comprehend a provision, they should not sign the Agreement until they fully understand and agree to it—after all, it is an *agreement.* If a buyer and seller have used competent counsel to draft the agreement and both parties fully understand the **ENTIRE** document **BEFORE** they sign it, they have complied with the third commandment of buying and selling a business—*thou shalt not purchase without a written agreement.*[3]

Commandment #4:
Thou Shalt Not Have Imprecise Books.

If you want a business that is prepared for a sale, run it like it is a publicly traded company. This may sound intuitive (and it is to a certain degree), but you must pay attention to where the money goes.

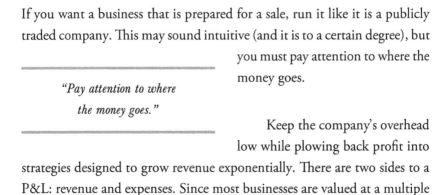

> *"Pay attention to where the money goes."*

Keep the company's overhead low while plowing back profit into strategies designed to grow revenue exponentially. There are two sides to a P&L: revenue and expenses. Since most businesses are valued at a multiple of their EBITDA[4], strive to keep the firm's EBITDA as high as possible.

Accurate books are imperative to a buyer/successor. Make sure the revenue and expenses going through the books are precise. Even though it may be easy to justify the trip to San Diego was for business, if it really was a two-week vacation followed by a two-day meeting, account for the meeting as a business expense and the vacation as a shareholder distribution. There is nothing wrong with mixing business and pleasure—just account for it properly.

Engage a CPA firm to review the books and prepare financial statements. Shoddy books reflect risk, and buyers despise unknown risks. Accurate books and third-party financials reduce buyer anxiety and limit *perceived* risk. Regardless of whether transitioning the business is just a few or many years away, run your books, and the company in general, as though it is for sale today. Maintain precise books that accurately reflect the company's financial story, and you are keeping the fourth commandment—*thou shalt not have imprecise books.*

Commandment #5:
Thou Shalt Not Stress Over Price

When it comes to buying and selling any asset, the price is nothing more than a math equation. In a business sale, the higher the revenue or the earnings, the more a company is typically worth. Nevertheless, remember what I wrote at the beginning of this chapter—*a business is worth precisely what someone is willing to pay for it—nothing more and nothing less.*

> *"The largest asset of a small business is its relational capital with clients."*

Every small business has value, even though they are built primarily on goodwill. The largest asset of a small business is its relational capital with clients.

As such, valuing a small business is an art form. It depends on numerous factors uncovered through due diligence on the part of the buyer and acknowledged by the seller. Valuing a business practice dependent upon goodwill is challenging. It is even more complicated by the fact most "firms" may not be firms at all. In the broker/dealer world, for example, the firm has no standing with the dealer or the regulators. The individual representatives are the agents of a broker/dealer. The transfer of registered representative's clients is subject to broker/dealer approval. What if the B/D refuses to approve the sale? Insurance agents are typically representing several insurers. What if the insurance company does not want to contract with the buyer, terminates the agency's appointment with the carrier, and the agency cannot find another market to place their client's business? Registered Investment Advisory firms, CPA firms, law offices, doctors, and other professional associations are also hard to value since they are equally dependent upon goodwill. Any number of factors can conspire against the sale of these firms.

The majority of investment, insurance, accounting, legal, medical, and other professional practices generate less than $500,000 per year in revenue. Many are one-man bands or solo practitioners. They eat what they kill and generate little net profit beyond the income paid to the principal. The only reasonable way to value professional practices is to hire a third-party appraisal company familiar with valuing similar businesses. As with real estate valuations, prices paid in the real world for professional practices are based on comparable sales of similar firms. Just like a 2,000-square-foot home in Laurel, Mississippi, is worth less than the same home in San Diego, as a rule, a rural practice is going to be valued for less than an urban practice. Unfortunately, there is not a *Zillow* either party can use to approximate a fair market value of the company.

The closest thing to Zillow in the financial services arena is FP Transitions (FP-T). FP-T provides advisors, based on uploaded financials, what they call a "Comprehensive Valuation Report" (CVR). The advisor can purchase either a one-time CVR or an annual subscription and request multiple CVRs at any time.[5] According to their website, "[The] Comprehensive Valuation Report (CVR) uses the industry's largest database of comparable sales of financial service practices to deliver a neutral, accurate, and market-based estimate of value. [The] CVR is used by advisors who are planning to acquire, or by advisors looking to sell a 100% business interest in an asset-based sale."[6]

Unless you have groomed from within or are selling to a candidate looking to buy an existing firm, most practitioners are selling a book of business, what FP-T refers to as "an asset-based sale," rather than an ongoing business. Most external buyers will likely be looking to fold the firm's clientele into their company and service the clients with the buyer's existing staff.

It is common for an outside buyer to ask the seller and the seller's staff to continue working with their clientele for a period of time. During this time, the buyer and seller will meet with clients to introduce the buyer and advise the clients of the seller's intention to leave. This warm handoff period also gives the buyer time to determine whether it makes economic sense to offer ongoing positions to any of the seller's staff.

When a buyer is looking to keep the practice intact, this buyer will often retain some or all the staff, relet office space, and may purchase the hard assets of the seller.

Either way, do not stress over the price. When it is all said and done, it is merely a math equation best calculated by an independent third-party appraisal firm. When buyers and sellers adhere to the fifth commandment—*thou shalt not stress over price*—the potential of closing the sale increases dramatically.

Commandment #6:
Thou Shalt Not Negotiate Financing in Arrears

Obviously, the simplest way to sell any asset is with a lump sum payment. Cash sales are clean and eliminate risk to the seller. But there is a problem: most buyers will either need or want to have the sale financed. Primarily due to the challenges of valuation, only a limited number of banks are involved in financing small business acquisitions. Not only are succession loans hard to collateralize—unlike real estate loans, which banks can easily sell to other institutions—acquisition loans are illiquid to the bank and become long-term assets of the financial institution. Furthermore, since the proceeds will not capitalize the firm being sold, as is the case with most small business loans, but are paid out to the seller, these loans do not meet the criteria set for small business lending. Unless institutions are comfortable with acquisition loans, they typically avoid them altogether. Consequently, it is quite common for the seller to finance all or part of the sale. Therefore, it is imperative the financing is secure before finalizing the agreement.

Seller Financing

Seller financing is a common way to buy a small business or a book of clients. Many potential sellers are reluctant to entertain financing the sale. Unfortunately, this reluctance to engage in seller financing is a big reason few small businesses are sold.

Seller financing allows the buyer to pay the seller over a term of years. From the seller's point of view, the ability to spread out payments through several tax years and earn interest on the outstanding balance may improve the seller's cash flow and spread out the tax impact of the sale over several years. From the buyer's point of view, seller financing allows the buyer to pay the seller out of ongoing cash flow. Since most seller financing does not include a pre-payment penalty, seller financing also gives the buyer who performs at a high level an incentive to pay off the seller sooner than anticipated.

Seller financing has potential drawbacks for both buyer and seller. For example, the seller remains tied to the business and may have to remain licensed, if applicable, over the term of the note. This may be good or bad. Some owners think they have the right to step in and "help out," even when the buyer is not interested or does not require the seller's "help." This reminds me of a sign in my father's auto body shop. It read:

Labor charge $50 per hour.
If you watch: $75.
If you help: $100.

For the seller, the most obvious drawback is the potential the buyer may default, pay late, declare bankruptcy, or try to renegotiate the loan in the future. Most seller financing agreements contain protections for the seller, including the right to take back the business, but who wants to come back and try to save a now-failing business? As a rule, the longer the payout, the greater the risk to the seller. While incorporating a seller financing provision into the Purchase Agreement is an option, many attorneys recommend a separate note and chattel mortgage against the assets of the business. Talk to your attorney about the pros and cons of seller financing from both the seller and buyer's perspective before finalizing the sale, because the sixth commandment—*thou shalt not negotiate financing in arrears*—is critical to the execution of an agreement.

Commandment #7:
Thou Shalt Not Misrepresent What Is for Sale

It is incumbent the seller properly represents what they are offering for sale. Do they expect the buyer to purchase their book of clients, or are they offering the entire business entity? Some buyers are interested exclusively in capturing the clientele (I would suggest most), while others are interested in the entity. The two conversations are quite different.

Buyers of a book rarely consider purchasing hard assets, leasehold, or keeping all the employees of the current firm. Their primary interest is in adding quality clients to their existing operation. Most sales of a client book are valued on a multiple of revenue. Buyers will want to know what revenue comes from where, and whether revenue is residual, recurring, or transactional. The type of revenue significantly impacts the valuation of the book. Transactional revenue is valued at a much lower rate than periodic recurring revenue. Lastly, if buyers are concerned key accounts may not be retained, it will dramatically impact what they offer for the book.

If the buyer is interested in an ongoing business, the computation of value is significantly more robust. These buyers are interested not only in revenue type, but the expenses they will be required to absorb after closing, e.g., leases, payroll, and other fixed expenses. Buyers of entities look closely at EBITDA, as well as revenues. Their offer will normally be based on some combination of EBITDA and revenue.

> *"The more confidence a buyer has that they will retain the seller's clients, the more apt they will be to make an offer acceptable to the seller."*

Buyer anxiety, whether of books or businesses, centers principally around client retention. The more confidence a buyer has that they will retain the seller's clients, the more apt they will be to make an offer acceptable to the seller.

Finally, if a buyer is interested in a book and the owner wants to sell an ongoing business, the chances of the deal happening are close to nil. The goals of the deal must be compatible for both buyer and seller. Be careful not to misrepresent what is for sale because the seventh commandment—*thou shalt not misrepresent what is for sale*—is easy to violate.

Commandment #8: Thou Shalt Not Stop Working Diligently

Some transactions fall apart at the eleventh hour because the seller checks out mentally before the sale is done. Occasionally, people in the process of selling stop doing what made the firm great in the first place. This is a big mistake. You will have plenty of time to hone your golf or tennis game after the business is sold. I know a car dealer who is fond of saying, "It ain't a deal until we see the taillights." Keep working diligently until the deal is done!

I have seen companies in the throes of being sold suffer a major downturn in business, and the sale collapsed. What happened? Often the founder took his eye off the ball, letting what made the company attractive to a successor fall by the wayside. Make the year you turn the company over to a successor the best year the firm ever had. Keep your eye on the ball!

At the same time, when getting the company ready to sell, examine what can be done to make the business as salable as possible. Do a time-revenue analysis. When owners do this analysis for the first time, they frequently find the firm is spending a disproportionate amount of time on a small portion of its revenue. Consequently, it may make sense to offload unprofitable clients or entire business lines before the enterprise goes up for sale. There are often firms which, through technology, can make what is unprofitable for one company profitable to another. Offloading usually means finding someone else to take over less profitable accounts. Consider:

- Hiring a salaried person to handle this business,
- Giving this book of clients to a newer producer, or
- Finding technology that can improve profitability.

My friend Rick's insurance agency exploded in value after his son, Ricky, exploited technology in ways Rick never considered. Determining the best use of everyone's time and focusing on what makes money for the company is simply good business.

While you are at it, try diversifying the company. I had a colleague who was proud of the fact she had a relationship with one client who represented 80% of her revenue. One day, the client, his wife, and his children were flying private and the aircraft crashed, killing everyone on board. With the entire family gone, her client left his immense fortune to a charitable trust. She had never met the trustee of the trust. The tragedy put her in a tailspin, from which she never recovered.

Sellers, do *not* check out as you prepare to sell. Make the last year the best year of your career, and you will never have to worry about keeping the eighth commandment—*thou shalt not stop working diligently.*

Commandment #9:
Thou Shalt Not Fear Selling Too Soon

People have often asked me, "Don, do you think you sold your business too early?" My answer is always the same: "Absolutely, but the only other choice was selling too late."

Most people wait too long to sell. Need proof? Go to a conference and count the number of people with not gray, but *white* hair. Far too many people have cessation plans rather than succession plans. The peak value of a company is much earlier than most people realize. Business value erodes quickly as the owner ages. The truth is, there are far more businesses that do not sell than there are businesses being sold. The older the seller, the less likely a buyer will pay top dollar. Indeed, value typically drops the most the year before an owner exits.

Most people just wait too long to leave.

Stephen Covey's first habit of highly effective people is to *be proactive*. Do not allow the decision to sell be a reactive one. By being proactive and selling early rather than late, the seller can dictate the terms instead of selling on someone else's terms. If a founder is passing the business to children, consider letting them take over before they need to rebuild it. In short, sell the company when it is at its best, not in a state of decline. I have seen men and women spend decades professionally managing the results of their business only to act like rank amateurs when exiting the same firm.

Unfortunately, when people wait too long, a serious health issue, the loss of a major customer, or some other currently unknown factor commonly becomes the impetus to sell, moving a business owner from a position of strength to acting out of a position of weakness.

I had a colleague who preempted the sale of his company because he stumbled upon a monster case he wanted to close before he sold his business.

The buyer was anxious to acquire the company and did not want to wait. The buyer suggested they close on the sale of the business and allow the seller to finish the deal. Assuming he closed his monster case, the buyer assured my colleague he would be compensated after the fact. The buyer even agreed to put it in the selling agreement. The buyer saw it as a win-win. The seller was not convinced, and he walked. Not only did he not sell the company, the monster deal never closed. The buyer bought another firm, and my colleague never found a successor.

The problem with breaking the ninth commandment—*thou shalt not fear selling too soon*—is you may never have the opportunity to sell late.

Commandment #10: Thou Shalt Be a Faithful Steward of the Business

Ownership is an interesting concept. The late comedian, George Carlin, in his monologue entitled, *Stuff*, famously said, "Everybody's got to have a little place for their stuff."

"The meaning of life," Carlin said, "is trying to find a place to keep all your stuff." Reportedly after John D. Rockefeller died, someone asked his accountant, "How much did John D. leave?" The accountant replied, "He left it all." One day we are going to leave this earth, and all our stuff is going to be left to someone else.

The truth is, we do not own anything permanently. We are just managing it for a limited time until someone else takes over. In the end, everyone has temporary possession of an incredibly small portion of God's resources.

Every individual is given a limited amount of time, a certain amount of talent, and an ever-changing amount of resources to manage. It is a choice as to how one uses the time, talent, and treasure they are asked to manage—a concept commonly known as *stewardship*.

The term steward is derived from combining two words—*stew* and *ward*.

Stew is a soup made with meat, vegetables, potatoes, and spice. The Brits called it a *stew* because it contained everything available in a kitchen.

Ward means to manage, protect, or guard someone or something. This is the reason patients in a hospital are housed in a ward. A **steward**, therefore, manages all the assets of a household, without possessing ownership, until the true owner requires them.

There is a statement Jesus made to His disciples that people have argued about for years. He said, "[No one] can be my disciple who does not give up all his own possessions."[7] The first time I read this, I thought, "Well, I guess I cannot be a disciple because it is not only a ridiculous idea, but no one in their right mind would ever do it." Now, many decades after reading it for the first time, I realize that is *exactly* what I need to do—give up ownership and realize I am a steward of resources that belong to God. I am granted, like all stewards, temporary custody of my *stuff*, as Carlin would say, until it gets assigned to someone else. I do not have permanent *ownership* of anything.

Once a person believes they are a steward, rather than an owner, it is far easier to *execute* a sale. Even though one may possess businesses, money, cars, houses, stocks, bonds, you name it, a faithful steward manages those assets for a time and arranges for someone else to manage them after they are no longer willing or capable of doing so.

When people operate from a basis of *ownership,* the tendency is to worry that they may not have enough. However, when a person operates on a basis of *stewardship,* their anxiety can be abated. Living as a steward brings freedom, respect, and happiness about succession instead of the dread many entrepreneurs feel over allowing someone else to take the lead.

As it turns out, the simplest way to move to stewardship is to learn to *give*.

Picture this: Imagine you are holding a wad of money in a clenched fist. For as long as you are gripping the money in your hands, there is little chance it will be lost, but nothing more can be added, either. Now, imagine holding the same wad of money in an open hand. While the money can fall out of your hand and be lost, how much more can be added to an open hand? Finally, imagine another person coming alongside and placing their open hands next to yours; then another, and another, until there are scores of hands pressed together. How much more can be added to these combined hands? Certainly, the bounty they hold collectively is still capable of being lost, but it also can be used to create opportunities otherwise unavailable as long as the now smallish wad of cash is held in your clenched fist.

Stewards do not fear what they might lose. Indeed, holding on too tightly restricts the movement and does not allow possessions to flow freely, back and forth between others, as stuff was meant to move. Indeed, the success of the one holding the wad in a clenched fist is achieved *despite* their lack of generosity, not *because* of it. Faithful stewards look for more and more ways to give. This leads to the greatest mystery of stewardship—the more the steward gives, the more they are asked to manage.

People love to talk about the need for faith when it comes to things like life after death and ignore the concept when it comes to life on earth. Faithful stewards manage resources the way a trustee manages another person's estate—without self-gratification. When a trustee manages the resources of another's estate wisely, the assets tend to grow, resulting in the trustee managing more resources on behalf of the estate. If the trustee manages the estate poorly, the trustee will be removed in favor of another manager.

Be a faithful steward of the business, and you will be keeping the last commandment—*thou shalt be a faithful steward of the business*—and will be granted the privilege to pass the stuff in your care to another steward who can commit to continuing what was built.

Play the Long Game

Like a trustee, it is wise to manage assets from a long-term perspective. I call this playing the long game. Trustees understand they do not have to own something to control an asset. The true beauty of a trust is it can manage assets perpetually. Trusts are a picture of ending with the beginning in mind. Trustees play the long game, managing the assets on behalf of multiple generations of beneficiaries.

Many businesspeople spend a lifetime nurturing their business. In turn, the business rewards them with income, wealth creation, and legacy. Do not forfeit your legacy. Be as professional about exiting as you are about building the business. Do all you can to allow what you built to continue into perpetuity.

Play the long game, and the commandments above will be a breeze.

For years, the competitive juices that spawned the business brought it to where it is today. Great businesses prepare diligently, fight competitively, and are committed to excellence. Now, there is only one thing remaining— one last act in the business. Play the long game and successfully exit with grace and purpose. In so doing, you are keeping the 10 Commandments of Succession and ending with the beginning in mind.

CHAPTER 12

THE PERFECT STORM

I n the fall of 2019, what initially appeared to be nothing more than an innocuous viral disease in Wuhan, China, quickly spread into the first worldwide pandemic in a century in a matter of months. A friend of mine was so unimpressed at the time that he named it the *Corona Beer Virus*. As everyone now knows, COVID-19 turned out to be a deadly pathogen that spreads like wildfire and is fatal when contracted by the wrong person.

Beginning in the middle of 2020, Dr. Anthony Fauci started referring to the "novel coronavirus" as the *perfect storm*. His analogy is spot-on. The original perfect storm, very much like COVID-19, did not look like it was much of anything until multiple converging events made it one of the deadliest storms to hit the northeastern United States in recorded history.

As I write this, at the beginning of 2021, the pandemic is still in full force. The virus's contagion is indiscriminate, reaching every sector of the public, from retirees to the most well-known politicos around the globe. President Donald Trump and first lady Melania Trump, Prince Charles and PM Boris Johnson of Great Britain, Prince Albert of Monaco, even my own brother and his wife have contracted the virus. Hundreds of thousands have succumbed to the disease. It is anyone's guess what the ultimate economic impact will be.

How will the pandemic affect succession plans? The answer will depend principally on how the parties to the plan *perceive* the pandemic's effect on the business, how much revenue was lost permanently, and if (and when) the business is operating at or above pre-pandemic levels. In many ways, the perception of the influence of the pandemic is as important as the tangible effect of the crisis itself. It has been well said that *perception is reality to the one perceiving it*. Perception is one thing, but direct loss of revenues and earnings is another. Across the globe, the virus shuttered firms in 2020. While some reopened quickly, most are not operating at full capacity, and others, especially those working in tight quarters, may never operate as they have in the past. It is clear the global economic impact of the pandemic will take years to sort out, but a person need not look beyond Disney to see how the pandemic can crush a business model.

The Impact of COVID on Disney

In early 2020, Disney was forced to close all its theme parks worldwide and suspended its cruise line indefinitely. Although some of their parks were allowed to reopen with limited capacity, the protracted closures of the California-based theme parks and truncated attendance at the other parks forced Disney to lay off over 28,000 employees across its parks, experiences, and consumer products division in the fall of 2020.

In a memo sent to employees in September 2020, Josh D'Amaro, chairman of Disney Parks, Experiences and Products, outlined the difficult decisions Disney had to make due to the impact of the coronavirus pandemic, including ending its furlough and laying off thousands of employees.

Due to the nature of the business, Disney has an inordinately high number of part-time employees at its parks, and the layoff significantly impacted this employment sector. Over two-thirds of the 28,000 workers let go were part-time employees. As of this writing, Disney parks in Florida, Paris, Shanghai, Japan, and Hong Kong are open with limited capacity, but California Adventure and Disneyland remain closed in California.

"As you can imagine, a decision of this magnitude is not easy," D'Amaro wrote. "For the last several months, our management team has worked tirelessly to avoid having to separate anyone from the company. We've cut expenses, suspended capital projects, furloughed our cast members while still paying benefits, and modified our operations to run as efficiently as possible, however, we simply cannot responsibly stay fully staffed while operating at such limited capacity."[1]

This was not an insignificant move, as the parks, experiences, and consumer products segment accounts for over a third of Disney's annual revenue. Disney hemorrhaged money in 2020. In the second quarter alone, Disney reported a loss of $1 billion in operating income due to the closures of its parks, hotels, and cruise lines. It lost an astounding $3.5 billion in the third quarter. Even a company the size of Disney can only absorb billion-dollar losses for a short time.

Challenges of Operating in a Post-Pandemic World

One of the biggest post-pandemic challenges will be what steps companies will have to take to restructure the businesses once they are fully reopened. Disney's financial woes during the pandemic were, as D'Amaro said, "exacerbated in California by the State's unwillingness to lift restrictions that would allow Disneyland to reopen." While governors in certain states closed only non-essential businesses and allowed for limited reopening, some state governments, like California, enacted far broader and stricter restrictions on businesses.

It is now clear companies around the world are looking seriously at the viability of remote employment in lieu of housing all or most employees in central locations. Working and studying from home will no longer be the exception. Open office environments and *bullpens,* where employees cluster in cubicles and other confined spaces, may soon go the way of cursive writing. Businesses housed in closed quarters, like banks, professional, legal, accounting, and financial practices, even medical facilities, may need to significantly change the way they operate in a post-pandemic world. We can also assume business travel will take years, if ever, to come back to where it was in the pre-COVID past.

Employers will not only be asked to reconsider their employment models; they will simultaneously have to modify the customer experience. How long will glass partitions be a part of the client-facing environment? What about safety measures? Will policies including requiring masks, sanitizing facilities throughout the day, rather than just daily, and touchless payment be the post-pandemic norm? None of these changes come without cost. Will businesses be asked to somehow absorb these costs, or will they be able to pass post-pandemic costs on to their customers? How much will profits suffer?

COVID is not only going to affect office space design, but the way people design homes will likely change as well. The use of individual and corporate technology will continue to explode. Lastly, we must hope that the government will neither downplay epidemics nor ignore pandemic prevention ever again.

None of these challenges, nor the questions they invoke, will be settled quickly. If the history of the 1918 Pandemic is a model, many people will be reticent about going back to pre-pandemic behavior for years to come.

The COVID-19 Effect on Business Valuations

What will be the effect on business valuations of small businesses, assuming these new ways of operating take hold? If revenues and/or profits drop, valuations will correlate their fall. No one is sure, but I believe *books of business,* as defined in the previous chapter, will still have significant value. I am not as convinced about the post-COVID valuation of ongoing small businesses. Those desiring to sell or otherwise transition an ongoing business, including its personnel and other overhead, to a successor could find fewer buyers and lower valuations. This will open the door for more cost-absorbing mergers, rather than conventional acquisitions, I believe. It remains to be seen whether successors will significantly discount valuations when they are asked to keep personnel, office space, and overhead required to operate the acquired firm.

Lessons from Prior Pandemics

Although many of us are treading in uncharted waters when it comes to navigating COVID-19, this is not the first time a virus has conspired to become a pandemic.

The AIDS/HIV Pandemic

The HIV/AIDS virus developed in the mid-1970s and quickly grew to become a worldwide pandemic. HIV/AIDS is still affecting the world nearly 50 years after the initial recorded transmission of the disease. According to UNAIDS.org, HIV/AIDS has taken the lives of at least 30 million people and is still newly infecting at least 2 million people every year. Although medications have been developed to safely treat those with the disease, it is estimated nearly 38 million people, including nearly 2 million children, are still living with HIV/AIDS in 2020. In one of the truly tragic twists of COVID-19, the UNAIDS website reports, "The lockdowns and border closures imposed to stop COVID-19 are impacting both the production of medicines and their distribution, potentially leading to increases in their cost and to supply issues. It has been estimated that the final cost of exported antiretroviral medicines from India could be between 10% and 25% higher than normal prices." The site goes on to report, "Recent modeling has estimated that a six-month complete disruption in HIV treatment could lead to more than 500,000 additional deaths from AIDS-related illnesses."[2]

One of the most important lessons learned from AIDS/HIV is sometimes viruses, even with the best treatments available, are unrelenting and can continue to plague the global community for extremely long periods of time.

1918 Spanish Flu Pandemic

The deadliest pandemic in the recent past was the 1918 Spanish Flu. According to Sam MacArthur, editor of MPH Online, "Between 1918 and 1920 a disturbingly deadly outbreak of influenza tore across the globe, infecting over a third of the world's population and ending the lives of nearly 50 million people. Of the 500 million people infected in the 1918 pandemic, the mortality rate was estimated at 10% to 20%, with up to 25 million deaths in the first 25 weeks alone. What separated the 1918 flu pandemic from other influenza outbreaks was the victims. Where influenza had previously only killed juveniles, the elderly, or already weakened patients, it [began] striking down hardy and completely healthy young adults, while leaving children and those with weaker immune systems still alive."[3] Over half of the people who died during the Spanish Flu Pandemic were aged 20-40. What is relatively unknown about the Spanish Flu was that it originated in the United States and killed more U.S. soldiers than died in combat in World I. For years after the Spanish Flu Pandemic, the fear of contracting the flu again had significant impact on the worldwide economy.

One of the key lessons we can take from the Spanish Flu is that pandemics can impact the political landscape for years after the virus abates. After the Spanish Flu Pandemic, people lost faith in the government. In 1918, the Democratic party lost control of Congress. President Woodrow Wilson, a Democrat, did not even contemplate running for another term in 1920. The Democratic party nominee to succeed Wilson, James Cox, was soundly defeated by Republican Warren Harding. The U.S. populace did not re-elect a president until 1936 when Franklin Roosevelt, a Democrat, was re-elected during the Great Depression.

While the outcome of COVID-19 is impossible to predict, the economic and social impact of the virus will certainly eclipse those of previous pandemics. The economic impact of global stay-at-home measures, as well as the closures of public areas, schools, and businesses is unprecedented. Many people have lost faith in government and are questioning, as they did a century ago, their handling of the outbreak. Nevertheless, the one truism of every natural or man-made disaster is the need to learn from these calamities by asking the right questions.

Learning to Ask the Right Questions

While pandemics come along infrequently, every year, powerful storms impact parts of the world. In 2020, there were so many named storms and hurricanes in the U.S., the National Hurricane Center ran out of names! It reverted to using the Greek alphabet for storms starting in September. In California and other western states, residents have

> "So, what do you do when the perfect storm, the fire, the hurricane, the pandemic hits you?"

experienced an unprecedented number of gigantic, forest-consuming fires in 2020. Thom Porter, the California state fire chief, told CBS' "60 Minutes,"

"A career fire [the kind a firefighter would see once in his career] was on the order of 10,000 to 50,000 acres. It dawned on me career fires are [now] happening every single year. Right now, there are ten fires in California that are 100,000 acres plus, and one that is 850,000 acres plus. Four percent of [California] is burned [out]."[4]

So, what do you do when the perfect storm, the fire, the hurricane, the pandemic hits you? Do you curl up into a little ball, quiver, and quit? Tragically, some people, when hit by a major event like COVID-19, never recover.

Years after Hurricane Katrina devastated New Orleans in August 2005, vast numbers of homes and properties remain unrepaired and abandoned in southeast Louisiana. When storms hit, it is easy to focus on *why*. However, I'm here to propose that the reason *why* the storm hit is not as important as the *what*.

- What can be done **before**, or in anticipation, of a storm?
- What can be done **while** the storm is raging?
- What can be done **after** the storm has passed?

These are the same type of questions businesspersons should be asking about their business continuity. People frequently ask, "Why do so few businesses continue beyond their original owner?" The answers are never the same. Nevertheless, there is often a common element—a perfect storm of sorts conspired against the continuity of the business.

Recovery from a Storm

I will never forget talking to Julian Good a few days after Katrina flooded his native New Orleans in 2005. Julian and his family survived the cataclysm but lost every physical possession in Katrina's wake. They lost their home, their possessions, even the family dog.

While Hurricane Katrina instigated the crisis in New Orleans, the city was destroyed by a combination of events conspiring to flood the city. While Katrina had exceptionally strong winds, the massive storm surge set the stage for the crisis in New Orleans in 2005.

New Orleans is extremely vulnerable to flooding. Much of the area around the city is 5-10 feet (1.5-3 meters) below sea level. During the hurricane, an 8- to 14-foot storm surge hit Breton Sound, where the Mississippi River exits into the Gulf of Mexico just east of the city. The storm surge swamped the system with more water than New Orleans had ever seen at once before. The municipality could not remove the floodwaters from the city, and the residents were forced to leave.

Six major levee breaches flooded the canals and the catch basins. Approximately 80 percent of New Orleans ended up underwater. In the process, the pumps failed, and New Orleans stayed underwater for about three weeks until the power was restored, the pumps and levees repaired, and the water removed. Julian's business (and everyone else's in New Orleans) was decimated. Between the storm surge, the storm, the loss of power, the failed levees and pumps—New Orleans became uninhabitable!

The Good family escaped to Atlanta, where they had relatives, as they pondered their future. New Orleans was deserted, and the Crescent City's residents were scattered all over the United States. Julian's employees were gone. His clients were gone. His city was gone. Julian could have easily declared that he was defeated. However, he refused to succumb to the downward spiral of fear, and instead trusted they *would* recover.

Julian was not afraid to return home. In fact, he was eager to get back! Sadly, it took four months before basic public services, power, water, sewer, and garbage collection were being restored, and people started to reclaim their homes and businesses. With his family in Atlanta, four months after the catastrophe, he returned to find a city he hardly recognized. His office was on the 36th floor of a downtown building. Without electricity, he was prohibited from entering the building until public services were restored, and the water damage was resolved. Cellphones were not operational for months.

> *"Instead of 'Why me?'*
> *his question was, 'What do we need to*
> *do to recover our home,*
> *our business, and our lives?'"*

Julian could have easily thrown up his hands, wallowed in self-pity, and asked, "Why me?" Instead, he went to work. Instead of "Why me?" his question was, "What do we need to do to recover our home, our business, and our lives?"

Four months after the storm, he went to work to recover. His home was uninhabitable, but he went to work to have it rebuilt. His business was non-existent. It took five months before he could hire a single employee. He did not sit around waiting for the phone to ring. He tracked down his clients and let them know he was there for them. In his own words, he went "back to the basics" and started over.

His word to his clients was simple—"How can I help *you*? What do *you* need?" This is an amazing principle of always putting others first. His is a classic example of the ancient Greek tale of the Phoenix, which obtains new life by arising from the ashes of its predecessor.

There are lessons everyone can learn from perfect storms when you understand they are:

- Inevitable,
- Opportune, and
- Purposeful

Let's look at the relation of these traits to succession and business operation in a post-COVID world.

Storms Are Inevitable

Most people, unlike the Good family, do not lose everything in a storm. Nevertheless, nearly everyone is asked to face challenges and controversy in their life. Like it or not, **storms are inevitable**. Life is a mixture of sunshine and rain, pleasure and pain, victory and defeat, success and failure, mountain tops and valleys. Martin Luther King once wrote, "The measure of a man is not where he stands in moments of comfort and convenience, but where he stands at times of challenge and controversy."[5]

Fifteen years before the COVID-19 pandemic, President George W. Bush was faced with a moment of challenge and controversy. Unlike what he faced during the 9-11 crisis, this was a moment of challenge and controversy requiring him to be proactive in averting a crisis *before* it hit.

Shortly after his reelection in 2004, the president read a book written by John M. Barry entitled, *The Great Influenza: The Epic Story of the Deadliest Plague in History*. While an obscure book, it predicted a pandemic was inevitable, and it mesmerized the president. In the summer of 2005, and against the wishes of many of his advisors, the president reached out to the author. Barry was a notoriously harsh critic of President Bush. To his credit, Mr. Bush did not allow Barry's public criticism to deter him from not only reading Barry's book, but speaking directly with the author and concluding a global pandemic was unavoidable.

Over the next four years, President Bush would spearhead the most comprehensive pandemic plan in global history. President Bush's global pandemic playbook included a global early warning system, funding alternatives, and a national stockpile of critical supplies like ventilators and PPE. Tragically, the plan was never fully implemented by President Obama, and it was ultimately eliminated by the Trump administration.

While it is incredibly easy to overreact during a crisis, it is equally hard to prepare for a crisis no one has ever seen. Unfortunately, a lack of preparedness for the perfect storm often leads to epic failure when it strikes. President Bush wanted the world to prepare for the inevitable, not be surprised by it.

There is an epic lesson to be learned from the COVID-19 pandemic. The inevitable global pandemic should not have been a surprise. It was forecast years ahead. While storms inevitably inflict harm, being prepared for a storm, rather than being caught flat-footed as the world was with COVID-19, needs to become non-negotiable.

In the same way, business owners need to make succession planning a non-negotiable. Unlike a pandemic or other natural disaster, succession need not be a crisis. Unfortunately, for many, succession becomes an inevitable business life perfect storm when they fail to take appropriate steps to plan for it. The need to decide whether to sell, merge, transfer, or terminate a small business is an inevitable decision every entrepreneur will face. You can either be prepared for it or surprised by it. The more prepared you are for this inevitable decision, the greater the chance your succession will not end up being a storm in the first place.

> *"The more prepared you are for this inevitable decision, the greater the chance your succession will not end up being a storm in the first place."*

Storms Provide Opportunity

If you have cared enough to have read this far, you likely care enough about the continuity of your business to see to it that it thrives post-COVID! In auto racing, when the yellow caution flag goes out, most drivers ease back, waiting for the green flag to fly, signifying the restart of the race. When the green flag reappears, most drivers are a touch slow getting back up to speed again—except champion drivers. The drivers who are champions are poised with their foot on the pedal, ready to ram it to the floor and shift gears with even greater enthusiasm once the race resumes. They are preparing to restart long before the green flag is waved by the judges. Their readiness to get a jump on the competition is what makes them champions.

Post-COVID, many companies will be even more successful after the pandemic because they had their foot poised to take the lead as soon as the green flag was waved. They feared neither the pandemic nor the restart. Champions use whatever is at their disposal to make their firms indispensable to their clients after a storm hits. They never stop reminding their clients they can help them recover.

Some businesses will not survive COVID-19. Other businesspeople will not *want* to continue. This will create a fantastic opportunity for bold entrepreneurs to purchase the books of competitors who either do not survive or do not *want* to survive. COVID-19 needs to be a wake-up call for many to put a business continuity plan in place. For others, it may remind them good health is a day-to-day blessing. They may now realize they do not have a lease on life, and there is more to accomplish outside their work.

Take time to determine the best way to preserve your firm. Look closely for opportunities available after the perfect storm to put the company in a position to succeed indefinitely. Maybe now is the time to merge with another group. Maybe now is the time to grow your business by the acquisition of other practices like your own. Whatever opportunities arise, when the green flag flies, be ready to put your pedal to the metal and wind up miles ahead, racing for the finish line!

Storms Have a Purpose

As hard as it is to admit, storms are purposeful. In fact, storms make you stronger and better in the end. Julian Good would not wish what happened to him on anyone. Yet, his recovery from Hurricane Katrina made him, his family, and his business stronger. Katrina tested his faith and showed him what he was capable of handling. Julian told me he would not trade the life he has now for the one he had before. He is a better father, a better husband, a better advisor, a better businessman, and a better person because of Katrina. Even though the storm was a freak of nature, he did not let the storm, nor the fear of recovery, put him into a downward spiral ending with giving in to angst.

The question, "How can a global pandemic make you stronger?" is one only you can answer.

The only way to truly live is to *live on purpose.* Everything else is just maintaining—existing, rather than living. When there are more years behind you than are ahead of you, the purpose of life becomes more precious than the life itself. It also becomes painfully obvious there are at least three questions everyone needs to answer:

- The first is a question of **identity**—*Who am I?*
- The second is a question of **significance**—*Does my life matter?*
- The third is a question of **influence**—*Do other people care that I exist?*

Most people go through life skirting around the questions of identity, significance, and influence. Too many find their identity primarily in their business and miss out on opportunities outside of *what they do*. Then, one day, something conspires to strip their identity away.

Others, in their search for significance, think their life does not matter. Nothing, however, could be further from the truth. Everyone matters! Tragically, over the course of my adult life, I have known six people who committed suicide, including my own nephew. At that moment, they no longer thought their lives mattered. When things became unacceptable or unmanageable, they ended their life.

Personally, my struggle has been with influence—do other people care that I exist? My identity has not been limited to my career, and I know my life matters. The last question is tougher for me. Influence infers leadership. Entrepreneurs generally find their purpose requires them to lead. The more you lead, the more you become a person who influences others and the world in which you live.

The Latest Perfect Storm

There is no question that Dr. Fauci was right. COVID-19 checks every box as a perfect storm. This virus is the most dangerous the world has seen in years.

As much as people hate to hear this, the experts have been telling us for generations that a pandemic was inevitable. While we did not know it would be COVID-19, the experts have been saying a global viral pandemic was coming years before the coronavirus unleashed its worldwide fury.[6] The real question is, are you going to let a pandemic, or something else outside of your control, keep you from doing the things you have perpetually ignored for years? I hope not, but the answer is ultimately in your hands.

> *"Are you going to let a pandemic, or something else outside of your control, keep you from doing the things you have perpetually ignored for years?"*

ABOUT THE AUTHOR

Donald is the author of two audio series entitled "Legacy Planning" and "Building a Great Business". For over 20 years Don's daily radio broadcast, God's Money, was heard on WAY-FM in southeast Florida and on the Internet worldwide.

Donald received his Chartered Life Underwriter designation (CLU) in 1981, his Chartered Financial Consultant designation (ChFC) in 1986, and his Accredited Estate Planner designation (AEP) in 1994. Lastly, he became an Accredited Investment Fiduciary (AIF) in 2013. He is also a Past-Chairman of Love without Boundaries Board of Directors (www.lovewithoutboundaries.com), a non-profit organization assisting orphans and vulnerable children.

A world renowned communicator, Donald has spoken on virtually every corner of the globe, including several talks at the MDRT Annual Meeting, the keynote to the first-time attendees of the 2000 MDRT Annual Meeting and was a main platform speaker at the 2014 meeting in Toronto.

He is the proud father of twin adopted girls from China, Sydney and Reagan. His wife Grace, does all she can to keep him home with her and their kids, rather than riding his bicycles, golfing, rowing, boating, scuba diving or skiing in the Rockies.

ENDNOTES

Introduction

1 Cerulli, U.S. Advisor Metrics 2018, Exhibit 8.01–Part 2. Age Dashboard, 2018, Cerulli and Associates, pg.232-233, 2019.

2 Shortly after this presentation and possibly even as a result of the presentation itself, one of the fathers soon realized he needed to relinquish control to his daughter. The father retired and entered into an agreement with his daughter to buy him out. The daughter merged the firm with another group and the firm is growing at unprecedented levels with her father's retirement and her being given the reins!

3 https://www.businessknowhow.com/money/nextgen.htm

Chapter 1: Providence

1 Read the second chapter of Philippians in the New Testament to get a complete picture of the "mind of Christ."

2 *The Peter Principle*; By Laurence J. Peter and Raymond Hull. Pg. 179. New York: William Morrow & Co. 1968

3 *If Things are So Good, Why Do I Feel So Bad?*; By George Barna. Pg. 210. Chicago, IL: Moody Press 1994

4 Luke 12:15; New American Standard Bible

5 Luke 12:17-21; New American Standard Bible

6 Mark 8:36; New American Standard Bible

7 Merriam-Webster.com/dictionary/psyche

8 How Much Is Enough? Money and the Good Life, © 2012 by Robert Skidelsky, Edward Skidelsky

Chapter 2: The Alice in Wonderland Syndrome

1 https://www.nationalchurchillmuseum.org/never-give-in-never-never-never.html

2 Covey, Stephen; *Seven Habits of Highly Effective People*, Part Two, Habit 2

3 Carroll, Lewis; *Alice's Adventures in Wonderland*, Chapter 6, 1865

4 Covey, Steven; *Seven Habits of Highly Effective People*, Part One: Paradigms and Principles

5 *The Brady Report*; United States Presidential Task Force on Market Mechanisms; Brady, Nicholas F. (1988). *Report of the presidential task force on market mechanisms* (Technical report). US Government Printing Office.

Chapter 3: Succession or Cessation, the Choice is Yours

1 Source – Ecclesiastes 3:1-8 KJV and from lyrics written by Peter Seeger for *Turn! Turn! Turn!* © T.R.O. Inc.

2 According to Encyclopedia.com, in Marxism, bourgeoisie is the social class who owns the means of industrial production. Their chief concern is the value of their property, the accumulation of capital and the perpetuation of their supremacy in society. Paraphrased by the author.

3 The proletariat is the wage-earning class in society whose only possession of significant material value is their ability to work. Marx calls a member of such a class a proletarian. According to Encyclopedia.com, in Marxism, the proletariat is consistently oppressed by the bourgeoisie, capitalism and the wage system. See Marx, Karl The Capital, Volume 1, Chapter 6 https://www.marxists.org/archive/marx/works/1867-c1/ch06.htm

4 Marx, Karl (February 1848). "Bourgeois and Proletarians". Manifesto of the Communist Party. Progress Publishers. Retrieved 10 February 2020.

5 Warsh, David; Knowledge and the Wealth of Nations, W.W. Norton & Company, 2006, pg. 65

6 Warsh, David; Knowledge and the Wealth of Nations, W.W. Norton & Company, 2006, pg. 64

7 Weisman, Mary Lou, The History of Retirement from Early Man to AARP, New York Times, March 21, 1999

8 Excerpted from https://gantdaily.com/2016/01/21/jack-nicklaus -golf-great-shows-nice-guys-can-come-first-in-business/

9 Jack Nicklaus at 80: The Golden Bear isn't slowing down; Palm Beach Post by Tom D'Angelo January 17, 2020

10 According to the US Census Bureau and Social Security Administration Data

11 Grau, David; *Succession Planning for Financial Advisors*, Chapter One, 2014, John Wiley & Sons Publishing

Chapter 5: Succession Matters

1 The **Form U5** is the Uniform Termination Notice for Securities Industry Registration. Broker/dealers, investment advisers, or issuers of securities must use this form to terminate the registration of an individual in the appropriate jurisdictions and/or self- regulatory organizations ("SROs"). The information contained on this form is public record and is viewable by anyone on FINRA's "Broker Check." Any "yes" answers to questions on a U-5 will usually delay the appointment of a registered rep to a new B/D until FINRA investigates why the question was answered positively.

2 Seligman, Martin, *Learned Optimism*, 2006, Vintage Books (Random House), New York, NY

3 Edited from 50 Success Classics: Your Shortcut to the Most Important Ideas on Motivation, Achievement, and Prosperity (published by Nicholas Brealey/Hachette, London & Boston) ©2004.

4 "Husbandry." *Merriam-Webster.com Dictionary*, Merriam-Webster, https://www.merriam-webster.com/dictionary/husbandry. Accessed 14 May. 2020

Chapter 6: Finding the Right Successor

1 See Joshua 1:6-9

2 Joshua 24:13-15 English Standard Version Bible – highlight added for emphasis

3 Taken from Numbers 13 of the Bible.

4 ᵐlok, Accessed from https://www.the-golf-experience.com/jack
-nicklaus-quotes.html on May 15, 2020

5 A GOAT is the "Greatest Of All Time"

6 This story is of unknown origin. It was told to me as a young man
over 40 years ago. I cannot attest to its certain validity, but I have always
felt it makes a strong point about how we should desire knowledge.

7 M. Scott Peck, *The Road Less Traveled*, Published by Simon and
Schuster, 1978.

8 Penick, Harvey; *Harvey Penick's Little Red Book*, Published by
Simon & Schuster, 1992

9 Goleman, Daniel; Social Intelligence: The New Science of Human
Relationships, Published by Bantam Books, 2006

10 Hill, Napoleon; Think and Grow Rich, Published by SCB
Distributing, 1937

11 This may come as shock to many of you but there are no golf courses
in Antarctica. If there were, I am sure Gary would have won there!

Chapter 7: The Five *Musts* of Succession

1 Maxwell, John; *The 21 Irrefutable Laws of Leadership*, 1998, Thomas
Nelson Publishers.

2 See article at https://www.successful-horse-training-and-care.com
/horse-reins.html

3 https://hbr.org/2005/01/how-to-play-to-your-strengths

4 The Rawlings **Gold Glove Award**, usually referred to as simply the **Gold Glove**, is the award given annually to the Major League Baseball (MLB) players judged to have exhibited superior individual fielding performances at each fielding position in both the National League (NL) and the American League (AL). It is an award handed out to players who had a superior fielding season. A total of 18 **Gold Gloves** are handed out each year with **Gloves** going to one player at each position for both the National League and American League. The winners of the award are determined by the votes of coaches and managers in the league.

Chapter 8: And ... One Must Not

1 Jerry's successor shared with me, confidentially, the details of the transaction. Not only was the deal fair, his successor paid more than fair market value for Jerry's business for three reasons. First, the successor felt for Jerry and wanted to help him. Second, the successor thought eventually he might be able to buy out the other advisors in the office as they came closer to retirement. Finally, the successor thought he could do vastly more business with Jerry's clients. During his due diligence, he concluded if Jerry had been more proactive in pursuing other lines of business with his clients, his production would have been significantly greater. In other words, the successor thought even paying a premium, the potential was too great to pass up.

2 Kim recorded rounds of 63-64-64-66–257 (-27) to win the John Deere Classic by eight strokes for his first career PGA Tour victory. Score was 10th in Tour history of 257 or better. The eight-shot margin of victory was the largest in the history of the event and tied Dustin Johnson (Sentry Tournament of Champions) and Francesco Molinari (Quicken Loans National) for the largest winning margin of the entire 2017-18 season.

3 https://www.mayoclinic.org/healthy-lifestyle/adult-health/in-depth/denial/art-20047926#:~:text=Denial%20is%20a%20coping%20mechanism,that's%20happening%20in%20your%20life.

Chapter 9: Familial Succession

1 See 2018 Business Owners Perspectives Study https://www
.massmutual.com/static/path/media/files/sb1020_final.pdf

2 The fair market value of the firm was estimated at about seven times
EBITDA, which is very standard for this type of agency. EBITDA is essentially net income (or earnings) with interest, taxes, depreciation, and amortization added back. EBITDA is one method used to analyze and compare
profitability, as it effectively eliminates the effects of financing and capital
expenditures. Rick and Sherrie agreed to less than half that amount.

3 The seven deadly sins are outlined in Proverbs 6:16-19. The author
is more poetic in his description than the list here, but the gist is the same.

4 This parable, found in Luke 15:11-32, was used by Jesus to demonstrate the importance of forgiveness, even when things do not appear to be
fair and certainly are not equal.

5 New Testament scholar Kenneth Bailey, who has spent most of his
adult life studying the social norms of the ancient Middle East, was quoted
in an article – see http://www.crivoice.org/inheritance.html - saying for a
son to request his inheritance while the father was still alive and well, was
akin to wishing his father was dead. He states in the article, *The Mishna*,
which is part of the Talmud and written about the time of Jesus, gives this
rule: "If one assigns in writing his estate to his son to become his after his
death, the father cannot sell it since it is conveyed to his son, and the son
cannot sell it because it is under the father's control." (Baba Bathra viii.7)
Even if a father decided to divide up his property among his heirs, neither
the father nor the heirs could dispose of the property while the father was
still alive.

6 Luke 15:29-32 taken from the New American Standard Bible®,
NASB® ©1960,1962.1963,1968,1971,1972,1973,1975,1977 by The
Lockman Foundation® Used by permission. All rights reserved worldwide.

Chapter 10: Are You Ready?

1   Murphy, Michael, Golf in the Kingdom, October 1, 1971, Penguin Books, London, England, U.K.

2   **"Mahatma Gandhi Quotes."** *Quotes.net.* STANDS4 LLC, 2020. Web. 18 Sep. 2020. <https://www.quotes.net/quote/8276>.

3   https://www.inc.com/scott-mautz/warren-buffett-says-you-should -read-500-pages-a-day-yikes-here-are-7-ways-to-at-least-read-more.html

4   Siebold, Steve, *How Rich People Think*, 2010, London House Press, Sourcebooks, Naperville, IL

5   Maxwell, John, Failing Forward, March 2000, Thomas Nelson Publisher

6   Harris, Blaine; The Four Laws of Debt-Free Prosperity; Chequemate International, 1996. The "Four Laws" are from the book. The comments are from a seminar Steve Scalici and I wrote entitled Five Years to Freedom.

Chapter 11: The 10 Commandments

1   Disclaimer: The author is not an attorney. The advice given herein is meant as merely a guide to prospective buyers and sellers. It should not be construed as providing legal or tax advice. Please consult legal and tax advisors before entering any legal documents.

2   **Oxford English Dictionary**, 2nd ed. (**Oxford: Oxford** University Press, 2004)

3   Disclaimer: This section is a very brief description of how a Purchase Agreement and seller financing often work. This is not intended to be tax or legal advice. When buying or selling a book of business or a practice, seek advice from a financial advisor, tax advisor, and attorney skilled in this arena. These are complex contracts, and every element of a contract must be considered carefully before signing it.

4 **EBITDA,** also known as EBITDA Margin, is the measure of the operating profit as a percentage of its revenue, "before interest, taxes, depreciation, and amortization," hence the acronym. Maximizing **EBITDA margin** shows the company's real performance. The higher the **EBITDA,** the more a company is worth in comparison to others in its industry.

5   https://www.fptransitions.com/membership

6   https://www.fptransitions.com/advisor_services/valuation-services

7   Luke 14:33 – *New American Standard Bible*. La Habra, CA: Foundation Publications, for the Lockman Foundation, 1971. Print.

Chapter 12: The Perfect Storm

1   Entire memo from D'Amaro can be found at https://dpep.disney.com/update/

2   https://www.unaids.org/en/resources/fact-sheet

3   MacArthur, Sam; 2020 MPH Online article OUTBREAK: 10 OF THE WORST PANDEMICS IN HISTORY published on https://www.mphonline.org/worst-pandemics-in-history/

4   https://www.cbsnews.com/news/western-wilfires-record-temperatures-california-60-minutes-2020-10-04/

5   https://www.keepinspiring.me/martin-luther-king-jr-quotes/

6   If you would like to read about how many people were predicting a global viral pandemic for decades before it occurred, read this article published in National Geographic in April 2020 just after COVID-19 was declared a global pandemic. https://www.nationalgeographic.com/science/2020/04/experts-warned-pandemic-decades-ago-why-not-ready-for-coronavirus/

CPSIA information can be obtained
at www.ICGtesting.com
Printed in the USA
JSHW041423260321
12871JS00002B/1